Nino Pernetti's Caffè Abbracci Cookbook

UNIVERSITY PRESS OF FLORIDA

Florida A&M University, Tallahassee
Florida Atlantic University, Boca Raton
Florida Gulf Coast University, Ft. Myers
Florida International University, Miami
Florida State University, Tallahassee
New College of Florida, Sarasota
University of Central Florida, Orlando
University of Florida, Gainesville
University of North Florida, Jacksonville
University of South Florida, Tampa
University of West Florida, Pensacola

Nino Pernetti's Caffè Abbracci Cookbook

His Life Story and Travels

around the World

Nino Pernetti,

Ferdie Pacheco, and

Luisita Sevilla Pacheco

UNIVERSITY PRESS OF FLORIDA

Gainesville / Tallahassee / Tampa / Boca Raton

Pensacola / Orlando / Miami / Jacksonville / Ft. Myers / Sarasota

Copyright 2008 by Nino Pernetti, Ferdie Pacheco, and Luisita Sevilla Pacheco

Printed in the United States of America on acid-free paper

12 11 10 09 08 6 5 4 3 2 1

frontispiece: Nino arriving in Frankfurt, 1964. Nino Pernetti collection.
color plates: photographs by Derek Cole

Library of Congress Cataloging-in-Publication Data
Pernetti, Nino.
Nino Pernetti's Caffè Abbracci cookbook : his life story and travels around the world / Nino Pernetti, Ferdie Pacheco, and Luisita Sevilla Pacheco.
p. cm.
Includes bibliographical references and index.
ISBN 978-0-8130-3230-6 (alk. paper)
1. Cookery, Italian. 2. Pernetti, Nino. 3. Caffè Abbracci.
I. Pacheco, Ferdie. II. Sevilla, Luisita. III. Title.
TX723.P3945   2008
641.5945—dc22   2007047537

The University Press of Florida is the scholarly publishing agency for the State University System of Florida, comprising Florida A&M University, Florida Atlantic University, Florida Gulf Coast University, Florida International University, Florida State University, New College of Florida, University of Central Florida, University of Florida, University of North Florida, University of South Florida, and University of West Florida.

University Press of Florida
15 Northwest 15th Street
Gainesville, FL 32611-2079

www.upf.com

I dedicate this book to my sweet, loving daughters, Tatiana and Katerina, who have taught me the true meaning of life. As all of us deal with our own mortality we start to think about what can be left behind to remember us by. It may be a scrapbook, pictures, a love letter, or a cherished memento. I chose to combine all these things in one package—this book.

It is my hope and desire that sharing my life's journey with you will, in some small way, make your love life and pasta a little better!

Nino Pernetti

CONTENTS

RECIPES

ACKNOWLEDGMENTS

I would like to express my special thanks to my coauthors, Ferdie and Luisita Pacheco, for their hard work in putting this book together. Kudos go to Ferdie for his wit and his Victor Hugoesque way of telling a story. My sincerest appreciation also goes to Luisita, who worked day and night for well over two years typing, editing, looking through and scanning hundreds of photographs and putting them all in order. She worked with me almost every day in the process of getting the stories and recipes in order, plus doing the flower styling for the food photo shoot.

Thanks also to Mitchell Kaplan, owner of South Florida's Books and Books and cofounder of the Miami International Book Fair, for his encouragement and advice; Gary Mormino, author and history professor at the University of South Florida, St. Petersburg, for his consummate knowledge of Italian cooking and his support; to the director of the Protocol Centre, Pauline Winick, for her tremendous help in correcting and polishing the book and recipes; and to Dr. Patricia Pardiñas, professor of literature and curator of the Chapelli art collection in Miami, for her gracious help in editing and keeping me in line with her precise corrections and sound advice.

Thanks to my good friends Gary Mason and Ron Paul for their support and encouragement. My gratitude to Bibi del Rincón for a sensitive oil portrait for the back cover of the book; to Albert Munoz of All Flowers, for providing the beautiful flowers for the photo shoot of the food; to Carroll's Jewelers for lending their special decorative plates; and to Derek Cole for his artistic photographs for the front cover and of the food.

Thanks to friends, to grant writer Alice Neji, to English teacher Merri Mann, to movie editor Tina Pacheco, to Bernadette Cunningham and artist Noah García for their help in proofreading and correcting drafts of the book.

NINO'S JOURNEY

Italy, 1958–65		
Limone	Locanda Gemma, 13 years old	
Gargnano	High School	
Gardone Riviera	Hotel School, Villa Alba	
Merano	Sent by hotel school to Grand Hotel Bristol	cook, busboy
Venice	Bauer Grünwald Hotel	waiter
Germany, 1965–68	*Learned German*	
Frankfurt	Möevenpick Restaurant	waiter
Hanover	First job with Intercontinental Hotel,	
	Prinz Tavern Restaurant	waiter
Meersburg	Lake Constance, Strand Hotel Wilder Mann	waiter
Frankfurt	Back at Möevenpick Restaurant	bar manager
England, 1968	*Learned English*	
Moretonhampstead	Manor House Hotel	waiter
The Bahamas, 1968–69		
Eleuthera	Cotton Bay Club	maître d'
Afghanistan, 1969		
Kabul	InterContinental Hotel, Pamir Supper Club	maître d'
Zambia, 1969–70		
Lusaka	InterContinental Hotel	maître d'
Livingstone	InterContinental Hotel	maître d'
South Korea, 1970–71		
Seoul	Americana Chosun Hotel	catering director/ assistant food and beverage manager
Mexico, 1971–73	*Learned Spanish*	
Acapulco	Americana Condesa Del Mar Hotel	food and beverage manager
New York, 1972		
Ithaca	Cornell University	summer courses

Malaysia, 1973		
Kuala Lumpur	Merlin Hotels	director of operations
Penang		for four hotels
Singapore		
Pattaya Beach, Thailand		
Belgium, 1973–74		
Brussels	Brussels Sheraton Hotel	food and beverage manager.
Turkey, 1974–76	*Learned Turkish*	
Istanbul	Istanbul Sheraton Hotel	food and beverage director
Venezuela, 1976–80		
Caracas	InterContinental Hotels	
	Hotel Tamanaco	food and beverage manager,
Guyana		promoted to regional food and
Maracaibo		beverage director for the
Valencia		four Venezuelan hotels
Belgium, 1980–81		
Brussels	Back with Sheraton Hotels	executive assistant manager
France, 1981–82		
Paris	Paris Sheraton Hotel	resident manager
United States, 1982–present		
Tennessee: Memphis	Holiday Inns International Division, corporate vice-president for food and beverage: South and Central America, Mexico and Caribbean division; Jamaica, Montego Bay; Bahamas, Nassau, Freeport; Aruba; Costa Rica, San Jose; Mexico, Acapulco, Mexico City; Chile, Santiago; Honduras, Tegucigalpa; Bolivia, La Paz; Venezuela, Caracas; Maracaibo; Brazil, Rio de Janeiro, Sao Paulo; Santos, Brasilia. *Learned Portuguese*	
Florida: Miami	Journey ends—Nino opens his first Italian restaurant Caffè Baci Nino opens his second Italian restaurant Caffè Abbracci	

INTRODUCTION

With the success of *The Columbia Restaurant Spanish Cookbook* (1995) and *The Christmas Eve Cookbook* (1998, with Adela Hernández Gonzmart), Luisita and I felt confident not only that had we covered a multitude of cooking stories from diverse Tampa families but that we had also told about traditions that make food the center of family life. But Nino Pernetti's *Caffè Abbracci Cookbook* adds to our storytelling because it is part recipes, part biography, and part travelogue, and it also showcases the determination and expertise of entrepreneurial restaurateurs. It is also the story of why Caffè Abbracci's customers have become undying fans.

In 1999 I suggested to Nino the idea of writing a cookbook that would capture the nuances of his cooking style. I felt then that the story of his restaurant and his life would make a dynamic book. He was intrigued but not interested at the time. Now he has agreed to tell his story, which is both captivating and unique. Working with him at our home in Miami was a pleasure. Luisita and I put our heads together and, using his voice, we hope we have captured his story and the many favorite recipes of Caffè Abbracci.

This book is much more than a cookbook. It is also the story of a young man's struggle to escape the poverty of postwar Italy and to achieve the success of owning his own restaurant in Miami, Florida. His expertise in hospitality comes from traveling extensively through five continents in top management positions with major hotel corporations.

Nino's most remarkable feat is his amazing ability to remember names: "Eat at Abbracci and you will never forget my meal and I will never forget your face" is his slogan. If you eat at his restaurant once, you will become part of his memory. He will know your name, your business, your wife's favorite dish, and your child's best story—a prodigious accomplishment.

Nino with Tina Pacheco on Tina's fifteenth birthday celebration with friends at Caffè Baci, 1988. Nino Pernetti collection.

His travels and adventures are the source of unique stories that can be told only by someone who has lived well and learned the art of hospitality firsthand.

By coincidence, or serendipity, if you will, in 1974 we both were in Kinshasa, Zaire, but we did not know each other at that time. I was in Zaire working as the fight doctor for Muhammad Ali in his world heavyweight bout with George Foreman. Nino was part of the InterContinental Hotel delegation sent to cater for the 70,000 people invited to see the fight. We were both caught up in the Rumble in the Jungle. Nino, a fight fan, did not get to see the fight.

Just as that televised fight is seared in the brain of every boxing fan, so will this collection of events, adventures, and recipes make a memorable addition to the food memories of anyone who reads it.

In 1987 my wife, Luisita, and I discovered Nino's first restaurant, Caffè Baci, in Coral Gables, when our daughter, Tina, was fourteen years old. She was working her first summer job at our favorite bookstore, Books and Books, owned by Mitchell Kaplan. We would pick her up and take her to Caffè Baci, where we met Nino. Tina celebrated her fifteenth birthday there with her friends. We loved Caffè Baci then, and now Caffè Abbracci has made us patrons for life.

Buon appetito! Enjoy!

Ferdie Pacheco

ONE

Growing Up in Postwar Italy,
1945–1955

Nino's Beginnings

Nino's childhood memories of the horrendous winter of
1948 in postwar Italy are his testament to the true silent
victims of that era. Why? Nino remembers clearly hear-
ing whispers that, at three years of age, he was about to
die. He caught typhus from his mother, Elda, who died
of the fever at age thirty-five. She left behind six boys:
Plinio, fifteen; Carlino, twelve; Diego, ten; Bruno, seven;
Olivo, five; and Nino, the youngest. The good people of
the small village of Campione, a place where everyone
knew their neighbors, were well informed of what had
happened. How could this happen? At the funeral they
wondered what Papá Vittorio would do with six motherless boys and one now dying. Everyone who came to
the funeral wept for this young family.

His father carried Nino to the nearest hospital, where
he was told his son's prognosis was bleak. There was
almost no medicine, little food, and life's little routines
and comforts had been forever altered. The hospital
was overcrowded with many sick and wounded. So the
doctors transferred Nino to Sant'Antonio Hospital, on
the outskirts of Brescia, for children doomed to die. On
a cold, windy winter day Papá Vittorio carried Nino,
wrapped in a thick wool blanket, into a carriage pulled
by two horses. Zia (Aunt) Idalia went along to comfort
her brother and her small nephew. The despair of a
father who thought that perhaps this was the last time
he was going to hold his baby boy was evident in
Vittorio's face.

Uncle Nino riding his bicycle,
Campione, 1936. He died in Russia
during World War II. Nino Pernetti
collection.

Mamma Elda and Papá Vittorio on their wedding day, 1930. Nino Pernetti collection.

Papá Vittorio with Plinio and Mamma Elda holding Carlino, Campione, 1933. Nino Pernetti collection.

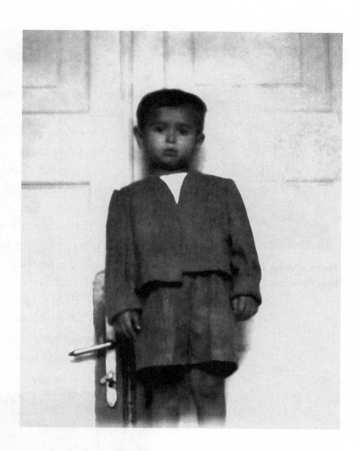

Nino at age three, Sant'Antonio Hospital, Brescia, 1948. Nino Pernetti collection.

Aunt Idalia came into Nino's room with a borrowed suit coat and short pants and told her brother, "We must take a photo of him. We have none; he is dying." Unable to speak and with tears in his eyes, Nino's father agreed.

Nino remembers the thrill of having a new coat even though it was much too big for him. The photographer posed him on a stool against a tall old lavender door. Nino tried to smile through his fear. He was taken back to bed, where over the next few weeks he miraculously recovered. He returned home within a month and was tended with loving care by his many aunts.

Mamma Teresa, Campione, 1948.
Nino Pernetti collection.

In 1948 Nino's father befriended and fell in love with a coworker, Teresa, at the cotton factory where he worked in Campione. She was from the small nearby village of Toscolano. Teresa's family did not approve of this relationship because not only was Vittorio almost sixteen years older than Teresa but he was a widower with six boys ranging in age from three to fifteen. But Teresa was in love and had tremendous compassion for the six motherless boys. She decided to marry Vittorio anyway and undertake the huge job of rearing and educating the children. For Plinio, Carlino, Diego, and Bruno it was not easy to accept a new mother, but for Olivo and Nino, Teresa was the only mother they had ever known, and they loved her.

Nino remembers his childhood as boisterous and happy. He did not know that his biological mother had died until a day when his overactive behavior in kindergarten incensed a nun, Suor (Sister) Giuseppina.

Cotton factory in Campione, 1951.
Nino Pernetti collection.

She was so upset at a childish prank that she blurted out, "What can you expect from kids who don't have a mother?" Nino was stunned. He did not understand what she meant. It was the first time he had heard this. Confusion and a great sense of loss gripped his mind and heart: "If I don't have a mother, then who is the lady bringing me up at home?"

Nino finally got an explanation from his brother Diego. The news was devastating, but a cavalcade of aunts, uncles, and cousins helped him realize that he was part of a huge, happy family. Today, my friend carefully points out that the sweet Teresa was, as far as he is concerned, his mother. Giving birth is beautiful, but giving love, as Teresa did, was the gift of an angel.

In 1950 she gave birth to Massimo, but it took her sixteen more years to add Lucia. Finally a girl had joined the family and was happily greeted and spoiled rotten!

The fluidity and ease with which Nino relates his story has prompted our decision to let him tell his story in his own voice. He is charming, and his story flies, page after page.

FERDIE: So tell me more about those early years. How did your family cope after the death of your mother, Elda, and with the additions to the family?

NINO: We were poverty-stricken. There was no hot water; we had no washing machine and no refrigerator. All the laundry was done by hand. Imagine. There were seven active boys who generated a lot of laundry. We were kept very busy. We all had our duties. My brothers were working with my father in the same factory, and it was low-paying employment. The factory processed cotton into thread. That was the only job everybody had because that was the Italy of the 1940s.

My mother's death was very difficult. The center of our family was gone. My brothers and father missed her cooking and caring for us. We sometimes had only bread and a bowl of *caffèlatte* for supper. But as rough as it was, my father believed in the importance of routine in our lives. We would eat exactly at the same time every day, at 12:00 noon and at 6:00 p.m., because food was important and eating together as a family was even more significant. We didn't have much, but what we had we always shared.

At school in Campione. Nino is the fourth child from the front, next to the window, 1949. Nino Pernetti collection.

FERDIE: What about your early years in Campione, when the summer months were over and you were home during the school months? How were those Catholic school years?

NINO: I remember it was hard work. Penmanship and the three Rs. I received a solid education early on. I remember parochial school was always over by mid-June for school vacations, and I still think the nuns were very tough on boys, but not as tough as our summers away from home. My father would send Olivo, Bruno, Diego, and me out to relatives in different places during the summer vacations because we had to earn our keep for food and a place to sleep. Our relatives were farmers. This was not a vacation.

Olivo and I were sent to Aunt Lucia's in the town of Voltino, high in the mountains above the lake. She was a hard-working woman of great strength. Lucia would get up every morning at 4:00 a.m. and begin her daily farming tasks by taking the goat to the field. She left the goat there and came back around 6:00 a.m. Together with her elder son, cousin Giovanni, we made it to the field in a carriage pulled by two cows. The cows looked like elephants to me, but the goat was a bigger challenge.

Then I had to take the goat back about 8:00 a.m. and I would have breakfast.

For me the most terrifying thing was when the goat would stop to eat grass and would not move. I kept pulling on her tail or horns to move her on, but to no avail. It was clear to me the goat and I were not going to enjoy the summer! I often felt like a Spanish matador, as the goat enjoyed charging at me; I spent a lot of time avoiding being at the butt-end of her stubbornness.

But one day I figured out that food was the best way to win the goat over. So I began to bring stale bread and cold slices of polenta for the goat. I named her Geppina and before starting our journey back I would give her a piece of each and talk to her. "Geppina, be good to me, be obedient and don't charge me and I will give you plenty of food, the kind you like, too." She loved polenta more than bread, but I kept the polenta for when I was in dire need to move her from the village's small cemetery.

Left to right: Aunt Diletta, Grandmother Teresa, Uncle Nino, Mamma Elda, Aunt Amelia, and Aunt Vittoria, Campione, 1927. Nino Pernetti collection.

Back row, left to right: Carlino, Plinio, Diego, Papá Vittorio, Bruno, Mamma Teresa. *Front row, left to right:* Olivo, Nino, Massimo in Campione, 1955. Nino Pernetti collection.

Like most kids, I thought the cemetery was haunted, and to get back to Aunt Lucia's we had to walk right by it. I was scared to death because the goat liked the fresh green grass in the holy field. When the goat stopped right in front of the main gate I was always panic-stricken. That is when I appreciated my new discovery of the power of food. The goat loved the polenta and stale bread more than the juicy green grass. To this day you will never catch me with a goat at a cemetery gate without stale bread! But I never told my aunt about my fights with Geppina. My reward was always fresh goat milk and her homemade bread with the jam that she had made during the winter months.

After breakfast I went back to the field and took cheese and water mixed with red wine to my cousin for his breakfast. I picked potatoes that were left behind as the fields were being plowed. All morning long we placed the potatoes in a container until, exhausted, we went home for lunch.

I fondly remember those family moments of my childhood, in particular, having lunch with Aunt Lucia, for her pasta was legendary. It was magical because it was homemade and had my aunt's special sauce. The entire pot would disappear in one second. Everyone fought for the pot and the serving spoons! I would devour my portion in a couple of spoonfuls. Then Aunt Lucia would bring out her special goat cheese. I never loved goat cheese as much as I did during lunch. Our dessert would always be a plump fruit from her orchard; usually, it was a huge, sweet peach. After that, we would take a nap and recharge our batteries for the rest of the long workday. To this day I am accustomed to naps.

For all the fun this life seemed to offer, I was very homesick during the summers because, from my aunt's house on the mountain, I could see the lake near where I lived. I could visualize all my friends playing on the small soccer field, swimming in the lake, or playing in the river. More important, near the lake there were no goats or cow smells! I could not wait until the end of

Olivo *(left),* Aunt Lucia, and seven-year-old Nino, Voltino, 1953. Nino Pernetti collection.

Six-year-old Nino, Campione, 1951.
Nino Pernetti collection.

summer to go home. The night before departing I could not sleep from the excitement of returning home to Campione.

The day before leaving, my Aunt Lucia would let me climb to the top of the tall cherry tree in the back of the vegetable garden and pick a bucket of nice, ripe red cherries for my family, plus a mouthful for me. At home everyone was happy to have me back. I always missed my brothers.

I did this every year until the age of nine. It would take me many years to understand the value of the tough lessons learned in this high mountain heaven of Voltino.

Then, one summer, my father told me that instead of going to the mountains I would be going to Peschiera, and that meant a different kettle of fish. Peschiera was on

the outskirts of the lake near the region where the popular Bardolino and Valpolicella grapes were harvested.

I soon realized why I missed my aunt's mountain. There I was high above my home, yet very near it. There I could daydream by looking down at the lake; I was in a faraway place yet not far away at all. In Peschiera I could not see the lake at all. While grape fields are less stubborn than goats, I was uncertain whether I would enjoy this new location.

FERDIE: You worked there long before the popularity of the Chianti wines, the Bardolino and Valpolicella wines, decorated the trattoria tables in their typical straw bottle. And as a child you could not have anticipated the gigantic shift in the wine industry that made Chianti a worldwide success.

NINO: Chianti's popularity was just a short year away. My relatives, however, were not in the bottling business. But, like a lot of farmers, they tended to vineyards, so they sent me to stay with the ones who were grape farmers. I hated the physical labor of the vineyards more and more; equipped with a pair of scissors I would cut the grapes, throw them into a container that I was carrying on my shoulder, then walk to the carriage to unload into a large oak barrel, which cows then pulled to the farm. It was endless cutting, loading, unloading. I had no strength in my hands because they were small, and most of the time the scissors did not cut well, so I used my teeth. Then, at sundown those of us too small to cart the barrels were assigned to the large oak casks to stomp and press grapes with our feet. It would be many years before I would smile at this sight. Why? It was like the episode in *I Love Lucy* where she presses the grapes, except then it was not funny; it was hard work.

In the countryside we would have lunch under the shade of a tree and listen to the balm crickets [cicadas] sing. It was hot and I was nostalgic for home. I was angry with my parents for sending me away from them. But in retrospect it made me a man; it taught me to value money—the liras then and the dollar now—to cherish work and the importance of food at work and home, and, most important, the respect honest working people deserve.

FERDIE: Those were tough lessons to learn. It seems to me that what you took away from those years of hard work was the warmth and caring that come from preparing food and sharing it with family and friends.

NINO: I make it a point to guard the time to eat with my family; it is the best part of my day. I make it a point to reserve that part of the day not just with my family but also to guard my wonderful staff's time to eat at Caffè Abbracci.

FERDIE: How and when did you begin your love affair with the food industry, Nino?

NINO: It was a matter of survival. I remember the winter months when I'd go with my father to paint apartments to earn extra money. This was done over the weekend, because the factory was closed Saturdays and Sundays. In those days painting was done by hand. One brush for him and one brush for me. All the furniture was moved back and forth, from room to room. We had to apply one coat of paint every four hours. Then we had to paint the rest of the rooms. We slept at the job most of the time, on an improvised bed. The lady of the house graciously offered us something to eat, but my father always politely declined the gesture, saying, "We brought our own panini." In reality, we just had a couple of panini for two days. I would look into my father's eyes trying to find an explanation. To my astonishment my father would say to me, "Never accept food from the family we work for because then they will ask you for a discount from the established quoted price." This thought never left my mind and I will never forget my father's "advice." But I also knew I did not want to paint houses for the rest of my life.

Education was compulsory only until the age of ten or eleven. After that, I had to apprentice at something to help feed my family.

When I finished parochial school at age eleven, my father quickly found me a job during the winter with the only butcher shop in Campione. The proprietor also had a little bed-and-breakfast where he rented rooms to executives and other technicians visiting the cotton factory. To top it off, he had the only trattoria in town, mainly for travelers. It was a good match.

Nino's sister Lucia, with our niece
Katerina *(on swing)*, Salò, 1972.
Nino Pernetti collection.

Campione soccer team. Nino is
standing third from the left, 1957.
Nino Pernetti collection.

Nino on bicycle with friends *(from left)* **Ciso, Nino, Gianni, and Sandrino, Campione, 1953. Nino Pernetti collection.**

I was the town's boy gofer. In the morning I would make deliveries and at lunch I would wash plates and glasses one by one with cold water, no dishwasher, and then went back to the butcher shop to sweep and clean.

Sometimes on Sunday, my day off, I would go to Limone. Limone is a characteristically picturesque village much frequented by tourists, mostly from Germany. It was a thirty-minute ride from Campione on my father's bicycle to visit my friend Vanni. His father, Signor Risatti, owned a bed-and-breakfast called Locanda Gemma, right on the shore of the lake. We would take the hotel's motorboat to water-ski. But one Sunday Vanni told me that we could not go out because his father had told him to work at the bar. The waiter who made the espresso had cut his finger cleaning a glass, so Vanni had to help at the bar. I told him that I wanted to help, too, so we could do the job faster and then go waterskiing. So off we went.

Upon our return Signor Risatti asked me, "What are you doing now that you don't go to school anymore?"

I replied, "I help my father do different jobs when he is not working his shift at the cotton factory in Campione. I also help Mr. Bortolino at his butcher shop and at the pensione-trattoria. I do a little bit of everything. But I don't like it because when I walk into the cooler to clean, it is freezing."

At that moment I told myself, "Don't tell me that he is going to ask me to work at the café permanently."

"Do you want to work here?"

"You have to ask my father," I said, hoping and praying that my father would say no, because if he agreed, I would have to ride my bicycle to Limone every day. Without a second thought, my father said yes.

FERDIE: By the age of thirteen you had apprenticed in the meat business and now, at Locanda Gemma, other doors opened. How was that experience?

NINO: My first real employment was exciting. The little café bar at Locanda Gemma in Limone was the place where men congregated after their lunch to have espresso and talk among friends before resuming work. It is an old Italian tradition. My job was to serve the espresso to customers. I also washed the cups and put them on top of the espresso machine to warm up so they would be ready. Then I prepared espresso perfectly for each customer. Signor Risatti noticed my open personality and my willingness to make the extra effort.

"You certainly have a great gift for pleasing the customers. You are going to go far should you choose this business," said Signor Risatti.

I rode my bicycle to work every day, half an hour each way, and I noticed that each day I made more tips. I wanted to make everyone feel good. Once in a while Signor Risatti gave me an envelope with money and said, "Give this to your father."

I always brought the money home and everything went into the family pot. Working there made me a careful saver. I didn't know how much it was, but my mother was always happy with what I gave her.

At Limone I was in heaven, but not only because of the opportunities the job offered, which I so enjoyed, but because of the family I worked with. They were as special as my own family. Being there made me appreciate why family shapes a man's soul. They made me experience new food, food that I had never eaten before. It was wonderful. I went from sometimes going to bed hungry to having an overabundance of food. There I learned to appreciate the essence of good food like veal scaloppine with delicious sauces. There was fresh fish from the lake, garden-fresh vegetables, and different kinds of meats. For the first time I tasted stuffed pasta, like ravioli, agnolotti, tortellini, all new to me and mouth-watering. This early experience was the beginning of my education in the delights of Italian cooking.

On July 12, my birthday, Signora Risatti surprised me with a cake and a little key ring as a gift with the number 13, which in Italy means good luck for life. I was so touched, tears came to my eyes. It was the first birthday celebration I had ever had. Because of our financial hardships, my family could not celebrate the small traditions that all of us take for granted, like birthdays and anniversaries. I never told my parents about the Risattis' surprise and kindness, nor did I share it with my brothers until many years later. I cherish the memory of that day as something truly special.

APPETIZERS

Carpaccio of Beef

Carpaccio di Manzo

18 ounces beef loin

½ cup mayonnaise

1 tablespoon grappa

2 tablespoons lemon juice

1 teaspoon Worcestershire sauce

1 tablespoon Dijon mustard

¼ cup Italian capers

½ cup minced red radicchio

½ cup minced arugula

Salt and pepper

If you have a meat slicer, freeze the whole loin, then cut it into thin slices about ⅓-inch thick. Place 6–8 slices on dinner plates. If you do not have a slicer, do not freeze the loin. Use a sharp knife to slice the beef into slices about ⅓ inch.

In a bowl, whisk the mayonnaise, grappa, lemon juice, Worcestershire sauce, mustard, and salt and pepper to taste until well combined. Place the mixture in a plastic squeeze dispenser and squeeze it onto the carpaccio in a checkerboard design. Place capers at each intersection and the radicchio and arugula around the edge of the plate as garnish. Serves 4.

Wine pairings: Jermann or Friuli-Venezia Giulia Pinot Noir; Beaulieu Vineyard Merlot.

see color plate 1

Carpaccio of Salmon

Carpaccio di Salmone

Fresh salmon, about 1 pound

2¼ cups coarse salt, divided

3 teaspoons cracked green peppercorns, divided

1 tablespoon raspberry vinegar

2 tablespoons grappa

4 tablespoons extra-virgin olive oil, divided

1 tablespoon minced fresh chives, divided

½ cup minced fresh basil

½ cup minced fresh mint

½ cup fresh minced Italian parsley

Juice of ½ lemon

1 medium tomato rose

20 arugula leaves, for garnish

½ cup sliced mushroom caps, for garnish

Cut 2 thick fillets from the salmon. Put half of the coarse salt on a plate. Lay the salmon fillets on the salt and cover with the remaining salt and half the green peppercorns. Cover with foil and marinate for 12 hours in the refrigerator.

Wash the fillets under running water. With a sharp knife slice them lengthwise into extremely thin strips. Place the strips in a ceramic or glass bowl. Add the vinegar, the remaining pepper, and the grappa, and combine well. Add half the chives, the basil, thyme, mint, and Italian parsley. Cover with foil and marinate for 5 hours in the refrigerator.

Remove the salmon from the marinade and lay on a plate. Drizzle with 4 tablespoons olive oil and the lemon juice. Top with the remaining chives and garnish with the tomato rose, arugula, and mushrooms. Serves 4.

Wine pairings: Plozner Tocai Friuli or Sauvignon Blanc, Sterling Vintner's Collection.

see color plate 2

Chicken Livers with Polenta

Fegatini di Pollo con Polenta

3 tablespoons unsalted
butter, divided

1 medium Vidalia onion,
quartered

¼ cup sweet Marsala

¼ cup fresh orange juice,
strained well

3 tablespoons fresh pink
grapefruit juice, strained well

1 pound chicken livers,
trimmed and halved, with 2
halves finely chopped

½ tablespoon cayenne
pepper

2 tablespoons chicken broth

½ teaspoon Champagne
mustard

½ cup all-purpose flour

3 tablespoons Cabernet

Salt and pepper

Polenta (see recipe, page 226)

In a large skillet, melt 1 tablespoon of butter. Add the onion and cook over moderately high heat, stirring occasionally, until golden brown, 12–15 minutes.

Transfer the onion quarters to a bowl and cool. Season the onion with salt and pepper to taste and keep warm.

Add the Marsala to the skillet and boil over high heat until reduced by half, about 3 minutes. Add the fruit juices and cook until reduced by half, about 4 minutes. Stir in the chopped chicken livers, and the chicken broth, reduce the heat to low, and simmer until the chicken livers are just cooked, about 2 minutes. Remove the skillet from the heat. Stir in the mustard and season the sauce with salt and pepper to taste. Keep warm.

Spread the flour on a plate and season with cayenne pepper. Dredge the chicken liver halves in the seasoned flour, shaking off any excess.

Melt the remaining 2 tablespoons of butter in a large skillet. Add the dredged livers and the Cabernet and cook over moderately high heat, stirring occasionally, about 7 minutes. Transfer the chicken livers to paper towels to drain.

Use ½ cup of polenta patted down to form a "pancake." Top it with the onion quarters and chicken livers, and drizzle with sauce. Serves 4.

Wine pairings: Dolcetto D'Alba Piedmont or Pinot Noir; Estancia Estates, Pinot Noir Monterey County.

Crostini with Pear and Prosciutto

Crostini di Pera e Prosciutto

2 ripe but firm Bartlett or Comice pears, unpeeled, cored, cut into 8 wedges each

½ cup mascarpone

1 tablespoon soft mild goat cheese (such as Montrachet)

2 tablespoons whole milk

16 ¼-inch-thick slices French baguette, lightly toasted

16 thin slices Italian prosciutto

4 julienned cups radicchio

Bring enough water to a boil in a saucepan to cover the pear wedges and boil the pears for 1½ minutes. Remove from water. Let them cool to room temperature.

In a blender, combine the cheeses and milk to form a spreadable mixture. Spread the mixture evenly over each baguette slice.

Place 1 pear wedge on each baguette slice and cover with a prosciutto slice. Serve on a plate with the julienned radicchio. Serves 4.

Wine pairings: Col d'Orcia Rosso di Montalcino; Francis Coppola Claret.

see color plate 3

Cured Beef with Goat Cheese

Rolatini di Bresaola con Caprino

1 garlic clove, finely minced

2 tablespoons minced fresh Italian parsley

3 tablespoons extra-virgin olive oil

12 ounces soft mild goat cheese (such as Montrachet)

2 teaspoons drained and finely chopped oil-packed sun-dried tomatoes

1 teaspoon dried oregano

1 teaspoon hot paprika

12 slices bresaola (air-dried cured beef)

Arugula

1 tomato, quartered

Salt and pepper

In a bowl combine the garlic, Italian parsley, and olive oil. Whisk in the goat cheese, sun-dried tomatoes, and oregano until the mixture is well combined. Add the paprika and season with salt and pepper to taste.

Place 3 slices of bresaola on each of 4 plates. Divide the cheese mixture evenly among the plates and roll the bresaola around it. Serve on a bed of arugula and garnish with quartered tomatoes. Serves 4.

Wine pairings: Vernaccia di San Gimignano or Chardonnay Clos Du Bois.

see color plate 4

Duck Foie Gras with Apple Purée

Fegato d'anatra con Purée di Mele

2 medium Granny Smith apples, peeled

2 tablespoons unsalted butter, cut in pieces

1 tablespoon Calvados

1 teaspoon raspberry vinegar

¼ cup Modena balsamic vinegar

2 tablespoons Italian red vermouth

2 tablespoons sweet Marsala

1 teaspoon sherry wine vinegar

½ tablespoon walnut oil

2 tablespoons equal parts minced fresh Italian parsley, mint, thyme, and chervil

10–12 ounces fresh Grade A duck foie gras in 1 piece

4 slices white sandwich bread, toasted, crusts removed

Salt and pepper

Preheat the oven to 375°F.

Place the apples in a small baking dish and scatter the pieces of butter around. Bake for about 30 minutes. Let it cool for 10 minutes, then scoop the apple pulp into a food processor or blender. Add the apple cooking juices, the Calvados, and the raspberry vinegar and purée until smooth. Transfer the purée to a small bowl, cover, and keep warm.

In a small saucepan, boil the balsamic vinegar, red vermouth, and Marsala over moderate heat until reduced by half, about 8 minutes; keep warm.

In a bowl, whisk the sherry wine vinegar, walnut oil, shallot, and herbs, and season with salt and pepper to taste.

Using a long knife dipped in hot water and dried, cut the foie gras crosswise into 4 equal slices about ½-inch thick. Remove any veins. Heat a large nonstick skillet until very hot. Season the foie gras on both sides with salt and pepper to taste and sear over high heat, turning once, until well browned and crisp but still pink inside, about 1 minute per side. Add the sherry wine vinegar mixture and cook for 1 minute, continuously spooning the sauce on the foie gras.

To serve, spoon the warm apple puree onto the toast, cover with a slice of foie gras, and top with the balsamic glaze. Serves 4.

Wine pairings: Malvasia delle Lipari or Vin de Glaciere Muscat.

Goat Cheese with Pine Nuts and Sun-dried Tomatoes

Formaggio Caprino con Pignoli e Pomodori Secchi

½ cup pine nuts

1 cup oil-packed sun-dried tomatoes, undrained

2 large garlic cloves, halved

1 teaspoon extra-virgin olive oil, plus extra for the bread

⅔ cup chopped, pitted, black Italian Gaeta olives, plus 16 pitted whole olives, for garnish

2 ounces soft mild goat cheese (such as Montrachet), sliced

16 ½-inch-thick French baguette slices

1 teaspoon hot paprika

16 Belgian endive leaves, for garnish

Salt and pepper

Preheat the oven to 350°F.

Spread the pine nuts in a single layer on a baking sheet. Toast, stirring occasionally, until lightly browned and fragrant, 4–6 minutes. Transfer to a plate to cool.

Combine the tomatoes with their oil, the garlic, and the pine nuts in a food processor or blender. Blend until smooth, stopping occasionally to scrape the sides of the bowl. Transfer the mixture to a bowl. Stir in the olive oil, chopped olives, and goat cheese, and whisk until smooth.

Toast the baguette slices. Brush with olive oil.

Mound the goat cheese mixture in the center of a plate in a timbale shape. Sprinkle the top with paprika. Surround with the toasted bread and garnish with Belgian endive leaves and whole olives. Serves 4.

Wine pairings: Bortoluzzi, Friuli-Venezia Giulia, or Joseph Phelps Merlot.

Mozzarella with Tomato Purée

Mozzarella Tricolore

½ pound ripe tomatoes

⅓ pound unripe plum tomatoes

1 tablespoon white cider vinegar

1 teaspoon minced fresh chives

½ celery heart

¾ cup extra-virgin olive oil, divided

8 ounces Italian mozzarella, sliced about ¼-inch thick

20 basil leaves, shredded

Salt and pepper

Place all of the ingredients except the mozzarella, basil, and salt and pepper in a blender with 2 tablespoons of the olive oil and blend until smooth. Season with salt and pepper to taste. With the blender running, add the remaining olive oil slowly, blending until quite smooth.

Divide the sauce evenly among 4 plates and top each plate with 2 slices of mozzarella. Top the mozzarella with shredded basil. Serves 4.

Wine pairings: Grego di Tufo, Campania, or Kunde Chardonnay.

Mussels with Smoked Beef

Cozze con Manzo Affumicato

40 large fresh mussels

3 tablespoons extra-virgin olive oil

1 tablespoon minced garlic

1 cup dry white wine

1 cup clam juice

1 cup fish stock

1 ¼ cup julienned smoked beef

2 tablespoons minced cilantro

4 bay leaves

4 large slices lemon

8 slices French baguette, toasted and rubbed with garlic

Salt and pepper

Thoroughly scrub the mussels and remove the beards. Rinse in several changes of cold water to eliminate any sand.

Heat the olive oil in a large, heavy skillet over medium heat. Add the garlic and cook until golden brown. Add the mussels and wine, cover, and steam until the mussel shells begin to open, about 6 minutes. Add the clam juice, fish stock, tomatoes, beef, cilantro, and bay leaves. Season with salt and pepper to taste and cook for 4 minutes. Discard any mussels that have not opened.Divide the mussels and broth among 4 bowls and serve with lemon and the toasted baguette slices. Serves 4.

Wine pairings: Muller Thurgau, Trentino-Alto Adige, or Chimney Rock Fumé Blanc.

see color plate 5

Mussels with Saffron

Cozze allo Zafferano

40 large fresh mussels

½ cup white wine vinegar

1 pinch saffron threads

½ cup extra-virgin olive oil

1 cup vegetable oil

¼ cup fish stock

½ cup clam juice

½ cup drained and chopped oil-packed sun-dried tomatoes

2 medium shallots, minced

1 tablespoon minced garlic

1½ tablespoons fresh lemon juice

½ cup minced fresh Italian parsley

8 slices French baguette, toasted and rubbed with garlic

Salt and pepper

Thoroughly scrub the mussels and remove the beards. Rinse in several changes of cold water to eliminate any sand.

Warm the vinegar and saffron in a small saucepan over low heat. Allow to steep as the mixture cools to room temperature. Transfer the saffron vinegar to a bowl and whisk in both oils. Set aside.

Transfer the mussels to a large, heavy skillet. Stir in the fish stock, clam juice, and saffron vinegar. Scatter the sun-dried tomatoes, shallots, and garlic over the mussels. Cover the pot and cook over high heat for 6–8 minutes. Remove opened mussels with a pair of tongs and set aside, covered. Discard any mussels that have not opened.

Taste the broth and adjust the flavor with lemon juice and salt and pepper.

Divide the mussels among 4 bowls. Stir the parsley into the warm broth then pour over the mussels. Serve with toasted baguette slices. Serves 4.

Wine pairings: Muller-Thurgau, Trentino-Alto Adige, or Sterling Sauvignon Blanc.

Oysters with Gorgonzola

Ostriche al Gorgonzola

¼ tablespoon unsalted butter

¼ pound mild gorgonzola

1 large rib celery, finely chopped

1½ tablespoons Worcestershire sauce

⅓ cup sour cream

½ cup fresh bread crumbs

1 hard-cooked egg, chopped

20 fresh oysters, shucked

Pepper

¼ cup minced fresh Italian parsley

Preheat the oven to 375°F.

Melt the butter in the top of a double boiler over simmering water. Add the Gorgonzola and celery and cook 5–6 minutes, stirring frequently. Stir in the Worcestershire sauce, sour cream, and bread crumbs, and season with pepper to taste. Combine well. Cool slightly, then stir in the egg.

Place the oysters on a baking tray and cover each oyster to the top of the baking tray with the cheese mixture and bake 8–10 minutes, until bubbling and light golden. Sprinkle the parsley on top of each oyster before serving.

Wine pairings: Chardonnay, Libaio, Ruffino or Chardonnay, Taz Santa Barbara.

Polenta with Shiitake Mushrooms and Gorgonzola

Pasticcio di Polenta con Funghi e Gorgonzola

½ cup walnut halves

3 tablespoons extra-virgin olive oil

2 cloves garlic, smashed

2 bay leaves

½ teaspoon fresh thyme

2 cups sliced fresh shiitake mushrooms, cleaned and dried

1 cup gorgonzola, crumbled

2 cups polenta (see page 226)

1 tablespoon minced Italian parsley

Salt and pepper

Preheat the oven to 375°F.

Spread the walnuts in a single layer on a baking sheet. Toast, stirring occasionally, until lightly browned and fragrant, 4–6 minutes. Transfer to a plate to cool.

In a heavy medium skillet, heat the olive oil over medium-high heat until hot but not smoking. Add the garlic, bay leaves, and thyme. Stir in the mushrooms and season with salt and pepper to taste. Increase the heat and stir constantly with a wooden spoon for 3 minutes.

To serve, slice the polenta and divide evenly among 4 plates. Dot with the crumbled gorgonzola and melt the cheese slightly under the broiler. Divide the mushrooms and walnuts among the plates and sprinkle the parsley over the polenta. Serves 4.

Wine pairings: Villa Antinori Red; St. Clement Cabernet Sauvignon.

see color plate 6

Polenta with Porcini Mushrooms and Italian Sausage

Pasticcio di Polenta con Porcini e Salsiccie

2½ cups fresh porcini mushrooms

2 tablespoons extra-virgin olive oil

1 tablespoon minced onion

2 garlic cloves, crushed

1 bay leaf

1 cup crumbled Italian sausage

2 tablespoons minced fresh Italian parsley, divided

2 cups diced ripe tomatoes, drained

2 cups polenta (see recipe, page 226; substitute chicken broth for water and add 1 tablespoon grated Parmesan)

Salt and pepper

Scrape the stems of the mushrooms gently to eliminate any soil; do not wash. With a dry cloth, clean the caps and slice them ¼-inch thick.

In a medium skillet, heat the olive oil over medium-high heat. Add the onion, garlic, and bay leaf. Add the mushrooms and the sausage, season with salt and pepper to taste, and cook for 15 minutes. Add 1 tablespoon parsley and the tomatoes and cook on low for about 2 minutes, stirring occasionally.

Slice the polenta and divide it evenly among 4 plates. Divide the mushroom mixture evenly and place it in the middle of each plate. Garnish with 1 tablespoon parsley. Serves 4.

Wine pairings: Dolcetto d'Alba, Ceretto Piedmont or Acacia Carneros Pinot Noir.

Scallops with Pesto

Capesante al Pesto

¼ cup pesto (see recipe, page 60)

2 fresh plum tomatoes, peeled, seeded, and chopped

¼ cup heavy cream

1½ tablespoons fresh lemon juice

1 teaspoon Sambuca Romana

¼ pound sea scallops, tough outer membrane removed

1 teaspoon extra-virgin olive oil, divided

Salt and pepper

In a small bowl, combine the pesto, tomatoes, cream, lemon juice, and Sambuca. Season with salt and pepper to taste and stir well. Set aside at room temperature for 45 minutes.

Rinse the scallops under cold running water, remove any dark strands, and pat dry with paper towels. Halve the scallops horizontally. Rub a large, heavy skillet with ½ teaspoon of the oil and heat until very hot but not smoking. Add half the scallops in a single layer without crowding. Cook over high heat until lightly browned, 20–30 seconds per side. Transfer the scallops to a bowl and cover with foil to keep warm. Repeat with the remaining oil and scallops.

Season the scallops with salt and pepper to taste. Divide the scallops evenly among 4 plates and spoon 2 tablespoons of the pesto on each portion. Serves 4.

Wine pairings: Vernaccia di San Gimignano or Simi Chardonnay.

Scallops with Saffron

Capesante allo Zafferano

16 medium-size sea scallops, shelled

3 tablespoons unsalted butter, divided

1 small onion, finely chopped

2 tablespoons dry vermouth

½ cup dry white wine

2 medium tomatoes, peeled, seeded, and chopped

1 teaspoon powdered saffron

16 small asparagus tips

3 tablespoons crème fraîche

Salt and pepper

Rinse the scallops under cold running water, remove any dark strands, and pat dry with paper towels.

In a skillet, melt half the butter and quickly sauté the scallops, about 2–3 minutes total, or until they turn opaque. Remove the scallops from the pan with the juices and keep warm.

In the same pan, melt the remaining butter, add the onion, and sauté about 5 minutes, until softened. Add the vermouth, wine, tomatoes, and saffron, bring to a boil, and simmer until the liquid is reduced by half.

While the tomatoes are cooking, steam the asparagus tips 3–4 minutes, or until crisp tender. Add to the scallops with the crème fraîche and season with salt and pepper to taste. In a saucepan simmer the scallops and asparagus 2 minutes. Serve on 4 plates.

Wine pairings: Santa Margherita Pinot Grigio; Alto Adige or Ferrari-Carano Chardonnay; Carano Reserve.

Seafood Salad with Red Bell Pepper Purée

Insalata di Pesce con Purée di Pepperoni Rossi

3 red bell peppers

1 onion, divided

1 tablespoon coarse salt

2 carrot sticks, peeled and cut in 1-inch pieces lengthwise

2 bay leaves

1 tablespoon peppercorns

8 tablespoons red wine vinegar, divided

2 celery ribs

8 tablespoons fresh lemon juice, divided

8 chunks each fresh swordfish and salmon

8 medium-size scallops, halved horizontally and outer membrane removed

12 calamari rings

8 medium-size shrimp deveined, shells and tails removed

8 medium-size mussels, scrubbed and debearded

¼ cup minced cilantro

½ cup tomato juice

Belgian endive, for garnish

2 tablespoon minced Italian parsley

1 medium cucumber, halved, seeded, and chopped

Salt and pepper

Roast the red bell peppers over a gas flame or under the broiler, as close to the heat as possible, turning often, until charred all over. Transfer the peppers to a paper bag, close loosely, and steam for 10 minutes. Working over a strainer set over a bowl, scrape off the charred skins; do not worry if a little stays on the flesh. Remove the stems, cores, and seeds. Do not rinse the bell pepper under water, because that will wash away the flavor. Cut the pepper into thin lengthwise strips then cut crosswise into ½-inch pieces. The peppers will release some liquid, so have a bowl ready to catch the juices. You may want to use the juices in the dressing for extra bell-pepper flavor. Set the peppers and juice aside.

Roast ½ of the onion with peel over a gas flame or under the broiler, as close to the heat as possible, turning often until charred all over. Transfer the onion to a paper bag, close loosely, and steam for 10 minutes. Peel; do not rinse the onion under running water or you will wash away some flavor. Set aside.

In a wide casserole half full of water, bring the water and salt to a boil. Add the carrots, bay leaves, peppercorns, 2 tablespoons of the vinegar, the other half peeled onion, celery ribs, and 2 tablespoons of the lemon juice. Adjust the heat to a simmer, cover, and cook for 10 minutes. Remove the vegetables and bay leaves. Add the swordfish, salmon, and scallops and cook for 5 minutes. Add the calamari and shrimp and cook for 2 minutes. Remove the seafood and set aside in a large bowl. Stir the mussels into the simmering water, cover, and cook for 2 minutes, or until the mussels open. Remove the mussels to the bowl of seafood and cool to room temperature; discard any mussels that do not open.

While the seafood is cooling, in a blender purée the roasted peppers and the roasted onion.

In a large bowl, combine the pepper and onion purée, the cilantro, the remaining lemon juice, the remaining vinegar, and the tomato juice and season with salt and pepper to taste. Refrigerate for 2 hours.

To serve, pour the cilantro sauce over the cooled seafood. Garnish with endive leaves to form a star and sprinkle with the minced parsley and cucumber. Serves 4.

Wine pairings: Renano Di Capriva Riesling; Chimney Rock Fumé Blanc.

see color plate 7

Shrimp with Fresh Beans

Gamberetti con Fagioli Freschi

1 cup fresh shelled white beans

1 cup plus 1 tablespoon extra-virgin olive oil, divided

1 garlic clove, crushed

8 fresh sage leaves

1 sprig fresh rosemary

16 medium-size shrimp, peeled and deveined

Juice of ½ lemon

1 tablespoon minced onion, for garnish

2 tablespoons minced Italian parsley, for garnish

Salt and pepper

Rinse the beans well under cold running water. In a saucepan, bring enough water to a boil to cover the beans by at least 2 inches. Add the beans and bring the water to a boil again. Add salt and pepper to taste and ¼ cup olive oil and boil the beans 12–15 minutes. When the beans are almost done, heat ¾ cup olive oil in another large skillet until hot but not smoking and sauté the garlic until golden brown. Stir in the sage and rosemary.

Drain the beans and add them to the skillet with the garlic, stirring to coat with oil. Remove the pan from the heat and cool.

Pat the shrimp dry with paper towels. Season with salt and pepper to taste. Heat 1 tablespoon olive oil in a skillet until hot but not smoking and sauté the shrimp for 3 minutes on each side. At the last moment, add the lemon juice. Stir and let cool.

Divide the beans evenly among 4 plates. Garnish each with onions and sprinkle with parsley. Arrange 4 shrimp atop each plate. Serves 4.

Wine pairings: Soave Bertani Classico Superiore; Veneto Fumé Blanc; Robert Mondavi Private Selection.

see color plate 8

Snails with Anchovies and Red Wine

Lumache con Acciughe e Vino Rosso

20 canned French snails

2 cups Cabernet, divided

2 tablespoons all-purpose flour

½ teaspoon ground nutmeg

3 tablespoons extra-virgin olive oil

½ tablespoon unsalted butter

1 garlic clove, minced

½ medium onion, minced

½ cup minced Italian parsley

4 oil-packed anchovy fillets, drained and minced

8 slices French baguette, toasted and rubbed with garlic

Salt and pepper

Place the snails in 1 cup of the wine with ½ teaspoon salt and marinate for 2 hours. Drain. Dredge the snails in the flour, nutmeg, and salt and pepper to taste.

In a heavy medium skillet heat the oil and butter over medium heat until hot but not smoking. Add the garlic and cook until brown, being careful not to burn it. Remove the garlic and add the onion and parsley. Stir in the anchovies and mash them with a fork to combine well. Cook for 3 minutes, then add the snails. Cook for 5 minutes. Add ½ cup Cabernet and cook until it evaporates. Add the remaining ½ cup of wine and cook for 5 minutes, stirring occasionally.

Place two slices of bread on each of 4 plates. Top each with 5 snails and sauce. Serves 4.

Wine pairings: Lagaria or Clos Du Bois Merlot.

TWO

The Sixties in Salò

Culinary Education

FERDIE: What do you remember of the 1960s in Salò, that beautiful area where your father built the family home after he retired?

NINO: Those years were my turning point. My father, my family, everything seemed to be a whirlwind of events. Yet, the house is perhaps why I am still so blessed.

My father retired at age sixty-five to Salò, a town seventeen miles from Campione on the lake. With his life savings he built a four-story house. It was a simple home, modest, but a fine place for all of us. The garden and lawns were not appealing yet functional, the gravel walks not at all pleasant to the eye but they efficiently led you to the doorway. The house was built for all us brothers so we could live together, and four of us— Diego, Bruno, Olivo, and Massimo with their respective families—still do to this day. Plinio and Carlino were married and already lived in Milan and Vesio, respectively.

The house was designed by my cousin Giacomino, who was studying architecture at the time. It was his first design project so it cost our family nothing. My brother Diego was an experienced bricklayer, so under his supervision and with the help of the rest of the family and other workers, the house was built in stages, mostly during weekends. While the house was being built we stayed in a rented house.

Papá Vittorio, despite the stringent and rigorous life he imposed on all of us, was highly respected and loved by all of the family.

Roberto Giuntelli *(left)* and Nino during high school break, Gargnano, 1960. Nino Pernetti collection.

Nino with high school friends, Gargnano, 1962. Nino Pernetti collection.

FERDIE: Nino, despite your youth, you realized that in order to advance in life you needed more schooling. If further instruction was to be acquired it would have cost money for your family because high school was expensive. There were roadblocks. First you had to get permission from your father. Except for your brother Bruno, none of your brothers had a high school education because the priority was to work. How did you accomplish it? Why was getting an education the turning point for you?

NINO: In those days to get an education beyond sixth grade was a big thing. Gargnano was eight miles from my hometown, Campione. To get to school you had to take the bus to another town, take your lunch, a panino with salami or parmigiano. You had to go properly dressed, and all of that cost money. I was afraid to ask permission from my father. But with my eyes wide open for improvement, I took the opportunity when we were at dinner one night to speak to him. Honestly, this looked like a scene from *The Godfather*. At dinnertime you did not know whether the atmosphere would be joyous, or whether it would feel like you were at a funeral, or just maybe normal. "Papá, I want to continue my education. You don't have to worry about the money; I will work on weekends at the cafes and restaurants," I said. I looked at my father as he reflected for a few seconds, which seemed like an eternity to me. With no expression on his face he agreed. I was thrilled. So for the next three years I went to high school in Gargnano.

Lino Treccani *(right)* and Nino with a soccer trophy, Campione, 1962. Nino Pernetti collection.

From left: Olivo, Nino, and Bruno, Merano, 1964. Nino Pernetti collection.

Nino's brother Diego, Giuseppina his wife, their baby Lidia, son Gioni, and Nino in Salò, 1974. Nino Pernetti collection.

School there was intense, except for rainy days. I rode my bicycle to school with my backpack on my shoulder and a newspaper under my shirt to shield me from the strong winter winds. I started out at 7:30 a.m., and back at 5:00 p.m., including a half day on Saturdays. During those three years during summer vacation I was still able to go to Limone and work at the Locanda Gemma.

At seventeen years of age, after I had completed the three years, the owner of the Locanda, Signor Risatti, summoned my father and suggested to him that I go to Villa Alba, the hotel school in Gardone Riviera. My father was reluctant at first. Despite my being only seventeen, he knew of my determination to reach my goals. Those three years were indeed the turning point in my life.

FERDIE: Serious advancement was in the offing at the hotel school. This represented your first real freedom. For the first time in your life you were on your own.

You were bitten by the love bug, but work and studying changed even the smallest details of life.

NINO: Yes, I was covered with odors. I always stank of onions, garlic, meat, and fish. And I was also covered with cuts and burns. I looked like hell; girls ran away from me. Although the kitchen staff was smelly and sweaty, I soon noticed the waiters' stiff, clean white shirts, clean black tux pants, and, above all, they smelled great!

Aunt Idalia giving Nino cooking advice, Salò 2003.

FERDIE: So at the end of the 1963 school year you were sent to the prestigious Grand Hotel Bristol in Merano, which was on the border with Austria. The school had a program to send students to the best hotels in Italy during summer vacations for further training.

NINO: Yes. I was mesmerized by the kitchen, which was probably cleaner than a hospital and run with military precision. The kitchen was not my first choice, but for now it was where I had to start. Upon returning to school I asked the headmaster to transfer me to the dining room. So the following year I returned to be a busboy in the hotel's restaurant, which was all white-gloved service. I remember the headmaster telling me that the job did not pay much but that it was a great place to learn.

The headmaster told my father that I must pursue quality establishments in order to progress in the hotel business and receive the best training. This sounded good to me, and by the end of my 1964 residency at the Grand Hotel Bristol, during the closing ceremony the general manager, Signor Gianfilippi, announced the best employees in the different categories. I was among the best five busboys out of forty-five. This was music to my ears.

White glove service, Grand Hotel Bristol, Merano, 1963. Nino Pernetti collection.

Nino serving champagne, Grand Hotel Bristol, Merano, 1963. Nino Pernetti collection.

FERDIE: Then the school sent you to the renowned Bauer Grünwald Hotel, one of the best in Venice. Was this another opportunity to escape?

NINO: This was one of the best hotels in Italy, and I felt the initial pressure. At the beginning I could not sleep at night; I was having nightmares. But I overcame all those fears in a short time.

One day the then-Shah of Iran, Mohammad Reza Pahlavi, was having dinner in his suite accompanied by his wife, Farah Diba, and his children, Ali Reza and Farahnaz. I was hypnotized by his wife's beauty, by her radiant dark-brown eyes and her grace. She was a beautiful woman, slim, with thick, black hair, a real queen. I was one of the three waiters chosen and assigned to the Shah.

While opening a bottle of wine, a very old vintage Bertani Amarone, I noticed that the Shah was staring at me with a pleasant expression. It made me so nervous that I was not able to pull out the cork. I did not have the strength in my small hands. The Shah noticed my nervous frustration and politely said to me in perfect Italian, "Hand me the bottle." I stared at him with great astonishment, and in one second he popped the cork. He said, "Yes, the cork was hard to pull out." He was gracious, with refined manners, yet appreciative of simple pleasures.

I remember that that night young Prince Reza was running around under the rigorous supervision of a Swiss governess named Helga. I saw the young Prince Ali-Reza Pahlavi forty years later in Miami at a small dinner gathering at the home of my friends Willy and Daisy Bermello, where I reminded him of the story. He was very touched that I had met his parents and his elder sister.

Nino *(seated in front)* with staff, Bauer Grünwald Hotel, Venice, 1964. Nino Pernetti collection.

FERDIE: You had an uncanny ear for learning other languages. By now you had a good knowledge of German, French and English, having studied the languages at school. It was a big advantage, although speaking it in the real world was a different story.

You decided after one year in Venice that it was time to further your knowledge of other languages and expand professionally. Germany would be your first assignment outside of Italy, and you went to the local newspaper stand and bought the *Frankfurter Allgemeine* newspaper and started to look at the classified ads.

NINO: I decided on Frankfurt because I had read Goethe's poems in high school. He was born and lived in Frankfurt in the mid-1700s. I found an interesting ad for a three-star restaurant that was going to open near Frankfurt in a newly constructed deluxe shopping center, Main Taunus Zentrum. It was the largest and the most luxurious in Europe. It was to open in early November, and they required top waiters and busboys. Since I was not yet fluent nor had I had enough practice in German, with the help of a German friend I wrote a letter applying for the job. A week later I received a letter telling me to start November 1.

It was mid-October, so I sadly tendered my resignation to the management of the Bauer Grünwald Hotel. I had time for a short visit home to Salò. During dinner I broke the good news to my father about going to Germany to work. He was scooping a big spoon of minestrone but put the spoon down. With the rest of the family on alert and prepared for what he was going to say to me he said, "You will get as far as Milano's Railway Station and the Carabinieri [Italy's Municipal Police] will arrest you for sleeping on a bench at the railroad station."

But I was already a mature twenty-year-old. I was no longer a shy, self-conscious child, and what he said made me mad. I would work hard, would succeed, and prove him wrong.

Nino *(second from right)* admiring a sculpture, Bauer Grünwald Hotel, Venice, 1965. Nino Pernetti collection.

Locanda Gemma, where Nino started in the hospitality business, Limone, 1961. Nino Pernetti collection.

SOUPS
SALADS &
SAUCES

Pasta and Bean Soup

Pasta e Fagioli

1½ cups dried red kidney beans

½ teaspoon fresh thyme

½ teaspoon fresh rosemary

2 bay leaves

1 teaspoon dried thyme

1 teaspoon dried rosemary

4 tablespoons extra-virgin olive oil, divided

2 medium onions, minced

⅓ cup minced Italian pancetta

1 garlic clove, crushed

7 cups chicken stock

2 medium ripe tomatoes, cored and chopped

2 slices Parmesan cheese rind

1 cup dried ditalini pasta

1 cup freshly grated Parmesan cheese

Salt and pepper

Soak the beans in 3 inches of cold water overnight.

Wrap the fresh thyme, fresh rosemary, and bay leaves in a piece of cheesecloth and tie it with butcher's twine; set aside. Drain the beans. Place them in a pot and cover with 2 inches of cold water. Bring the water to a boil, then lower the heat and simmer the beans until they are tender, about 2 minutes. Drain and rinse the beans under cold water.

Heat 2 tablespoons of the olive oil in a large, heavy saucepan; add the onion, pancetta, and garlic, and sauté until the onion is browned, 7–9 minutes. Add the chicken stock, tomatoes, beans, and the herb bundle. Cover and bring to a boil over high heat. Lower the heat, add the Parmesan rinds, and simmer for 30 minutes. Remove the herb bundle with a slotted spoon and discard. Remove half of the beans and purée them until smooth in a blender or food processor. Return the purée to the soup. Cover and return the soup to a boil over high heat. Add the pasta, cover, and boil, stirring occasionally, until the pasta is tender but still firm to the bite, about 10 minutes. Remove the pan from the heat, season with salt and pepper to taste, and allow the soup to rest for 10–12 minutes. Remove the Parmesan rinds and cut them into 12 small squares.

Ladle the soup into 6 bowls, add 2 pieces of Parmesan rind to each, and vigorously stir in the grated Parmesan. Drizzle the remaining olive oil over each serving. Serves 6.

Wine pairings: Col d'Orcia Rosso di Montalcino; Estancia Estates Pinot Noir.

Fish Soup

Zuppa di Pesce

1 bay leaf

1 celery rib, julienned

1 fresh rosemary sprig

1 medium carrot, julienned

1 fresh thyme sprig

¼ cup extra-virgin olive oil

1 medium red onion, finely chopped

5 garlic cloves, 4 thinly sliced, 1 left whole

½ tablespoon red pepper flakes

¾ cup minced fresh Italian parsley

2 14–ounce cans peeled tomatoes in juice

1 cup dry white wine

2 cups fish stock

1 cup clam juice

3 tablespoons concentrated Italian tomato paste (in a tube)

12 littleneck clams, scrubbed

12 medium mussels, scrubbed, debearded, and rinsed

1 cup peeled and diced red potatoes

2 pounds mixed fish (salmon, tuna, swordfish, calamari), cut in ¾-inch chunks

1 pound medium shrimp, peeled and deveined

2 loaves French baguette, cut into 16 slices, toasted and rubbed with garlic

Salt and pepper

Put the bay leaf, celery, rosemary, carrot, and thyme in a cheesecloth bag. Tie with butcher's twine and set aside.

In a large Dutch oven, heat the olive oil over medium heat until almost smoking. Add the onions, garlic, red pepper flakes, and parsley and cook until the onion is translucent, 6–8 minutes. Add the tomatoes and their juice, the wine, fish stock, clam juice, and the herb bundle. Stir in the tomato paste. Cover and simmer for 12 minutes. Add the clams to the pot, cover, and cook, about 10 minutes. Remove the clams to a bowl, discarding any that have not opened, and keep them warm. Repeat with the mussels. Add the potatoes and simmer about 10 minutes. Add the fish and shrimp, lower the heat, cover, and simmer for 6–8 minutes. Return the clams and mussels to the pot and remove the vegetable bundle. Season with salt and pepper to taste and stir a few times.

Divide the fish and seafood evenly among 4 warmed bowls, then pour the stock over them. Serve immediately with the bread. Serves 4.

Wine pairings: Vigne de Leon, Tocai; Gregich Hills Fumé Blanc.

Chilled Tomato Soup and Roasted Garlic

Zuppa Fredda di Pomodoro e Aglio

6 garlic cloves, unpeeled

3 pounds vine-ripened tomatoes, quartered

2 tablespoons Modena balsamic vinegar

1 yellow bell pepper, seeded and diced

1 cup peeled and diced gherkins (small cucumbers)

2 tablespoons fresh lemon juice

2 tablespoons canola oil

3 tablespoons extra-virgin olive oil

16 chives

Salt and pepper

In a small heavy skillet dry-roast the garlic over moderately low heat, turning occasionally, until the skin is browned and garlic is tender, about 25 minutes; peel. In a blender purée the garlic and tomatoes in batches and force through a fine sieve into a bowl. Stir in the balsamic vinegar and season with salt and pepper to taste. Refrigerate the soup, covered, until cold, approximately 2 hours.

Combine the bell pepper, gherkins, and lemon juice. Blend in the canola oil and toss to mix. Refrigerate, covered, while preparing the rest of the salad.

Mix the tomato purée with the olive oil. Divide the purée equally among 6 soup bowls. Spoon the bell pepper mixture in the center of each bowl. Garnish with the chives. Serves 6.

Wine pairings: Trentino-Alto Adige Muller Thurgau; Sonoma-Cutrer or Chardonnay.

Tomato Soup with Two Cheeses

Crema di Pomodoro ai Due Formaggi

2 pounds ripe tomatoes

6 sprigs fresh rosemary

6 sprigs fresh thyme

3 garlic cloves, chopped

½ teaspoon sugar

6 tablespoons extra-virgin olive oil, divided

¾ cup mascarpone cheese

½ cup freshly grated Pecorino cheese

1 cup minced onions

⅔ cup minced carrots

4 cups chicken stock

Croutons:

½ cup unsalted butter

½ cup extra-virgin olive oil

2 tablespoons minced garlic

4 cups day-old French baguette, cut into ¾-inch cubes

Salt and pepper

Preheat the oven to 275°F. Line a large baking sheet with parchment paper.

Slice ¼ to ½ inch off the top of each tomato. Sprinkle each tomato with rosemary, thyme, garlic, and sugar. Season with salt and pepper to taste and drizzle with 4 tablespoons olive oil. Roast about 3 hours, or until the tomatoes are cooked and some of the skins have burst.

In a small bowl combine the mascarpone and Pecorino cheeses until smooth. Refrigerate.

Force the roasted tomatoes through a tomato press or a food mill. Heat 2 tablespoons olive oil in a heavy Dutch oven over medium heat until hot but not smoking. Add the onions and carrots and stir until the vegetables begin to soften, 4–6 minutes. Add the tomatoes and chicken stock and simmer for 6 minutes. Purée the soup in batches in a blender. Return the soup to the Dutch oven. Season with salt and pepper to taste.

For the croutons, in a large sauté pan, melt the butter in ½ cup olive oil over medium-low heat. Add the garlic and bread cubes and toss until the bread pieces are well coated. Reduce the heat to low or transfer the bread to a preheated 350°F oven and cook, stirring or turning frequently, until the bread is golden on all sides, about 25 minutes. Transfer the bread to paper towels to drain and cool. Do not refrigerate.

Divide the soup evenly among 6 warmed bowls and top each with a scoop of the cheese mixture and croutons. Serves 6.

Wine pairings: Col d'Orcia Rosso di Montalcino; Estancia Estates Pinot Noir.

Tomato and Lentil Soup

Zuppa di Pomodoro e Lenticchie

6 ripe tomatoes

2½ tablespoons extra-virgin olive oil, plus extra for drizzling

1 small onion, minced

2 cloves garlic, minced

3 tablespoons concentrated Italian tomato paste (in tube)

3 cups brown lentils, soaked overnight and drained

7 cups chicken stock

Salt and pepper

Bring a large pot of water to a boil. Make a cross-shaped slit on the bottom of each tomato and blanch them for 2 minutes in boiling water. Plunge the tomatoes into an ice water bath to stop cooking and drain. Remove the peel, squeeze out the seeds, and remove and discard the core. Chop and set aside.

In a pan over medium heat, warm 2½ tablespoons olive oil. Add the onion and sauté for 3 minutes. Add the garlic and tomatoes and sauté for 4 minutes. Add the tomato paste and lentils, stirring to coat the ingredients with the tomato paste. Pour in the stock, season with salt and pepper to taste, and stir. Cover and cook over medium heat for 35 minutes to allow the flavors to blend and the lentils to soften.

Ladle the soup into 6 bowls. To serve, drizzle with olive oil. Serves 6.

Wine pairings: Col d'Orcia Rosso di Montalcino; Estancia Estates Pinot Noir.

Zucchini Soup

Zuppa di Zucchini

2 tablespoons extra-virgin olive oil

2½ tablespoons unsalted butter

2 celery ribs, peeled and diced

1 small carrot, peeled and sliced

1 small onion, minced

1 bay leaf

½ cup minced fresh Italian parsley

¼ teaspoon minced fresh thyme

1 pound small zucchini, diced

½ cup cream

2½ cups chicken stock

2 cups croutons (see recipe, page 54)

Salt and pepper

In a large, heavy saucepan, heat the olive oil and butter until hot but not smoking. Stir in the celery, carrot, onion, bay leaf, parsley, and thyme and cook over low heat, stirring occasionally, until the onion is translucent, about 20 minutes. Increase the heat to moderate. Stir in the zucchini, cream, and chicken stock, season with salt and pepper to taste, and simmer the soup until the zucchini is soft, about 10 minutes. Discard the bay leaf.

Working in batches, purée the soup in a blender until smooth. Return the soup to the saucepan and reheat gently. Season with salt and pepper to taste. Spoon the soup into warmed bowls and sprinkle with croutons. Serves 6.

Wine pairing: Lagaria, Sicilia, Sterling Chardonnay.

Mozzarella and Potato Salad

Insalata di Mozzarella e Patate

3 pounds medium red-skinned potatoes

1 tablespoon coarse salt

2 cups diced Italian mozzarella

2 cups cherry tomatoes, halved

2 tablespoons Modena balsamic vinegar

2 cups tomato vinaigrette (see recipe, page 60)

Salt and pepper

Wash the potatoes under cold running water, scrubbing well to remove all traces of soil. Place them in a large pot and add cold water to cover by 2 inches. Remove the potatoes, add the coarse salt to the water, and bring to a boil over moderately high heat. Add the potatoes and boil for 15–20 minutes. Drain and cool in ice water. Peel the potatoes, slice them ¼-inch thick, and place them in a large bowl. Stir in the mozzarella, cherry tomatoes, balsamic vinegar, and tomato vinaigrette and toss well. Season with salt and pepper to taste. Serves 4.

Wine pairings: Dolcetto di Diano d'Alba; Kunde Estate Merlot.

Pear and Goat Cheese Salad

Insalata di Pera e Formaggio Caprino

¼ cup sliced almonds

1 ripe but firm peeled Bartlett or Comice pear

1 quart water

4 cups packed mesclun greens

¼ cup crumbled soft mild goat cheese (such as Montrachet)

½ cup extra-virgin olive oil

¼ cup raspberry vinegar

Salt and pepper

Preheat the oven to 400°F.

Line a baking sheet with parchment paper and toast the almonds for 10 minutes, shaking the baking sheet frequently.

Place the whole pear in a quart of water and bring to a boil. Lower the heat to moderate and cook the pear for 2 minutes. Remove the pear and cool. Dice the cooled pear.

In a large bowl, combine the greens, diced pear, goat cheese, olive oil, and raspberry vinegar. Toss well, season with salt and pepper to taste, and divide evenly among 4 salad plates. Top with the almonds. Serves 4.

Wine pairings: Trentino–Alto Adige Muller Thurgau, Heitz Cellar Select Chardonnay.

Béchamel Sauce

Salsa Beschiamella

3 cups whole milk

Salt

6 black peppercorns, crushed

Pinch freshly grated nutmeg

1 bay leaf

3 tablespoons unsalted butter

⅓ cup all-purpose flour

⅓ cup freshly grated
Parmesan cheese

Pour the milk into a saucepan, season with salt to taste, and add the peppercorns, nutmeg, and bay leaf. Cook over medium-low heat until bubbles form around the edge. Remove the pan from the heat and keep warm.

Meanwhile, melt the butter in another heavy saucepan over medium heat. When it starts to foam, add the flour and whisk continuously until smooth, 4–6 minutes. Pour the milk into the flour mixture in a steady stream, whisking constantly. Cook until the sauce thickens. Remove from the heat and whisk in the Parmesan cheese. Strain the sauce through a fine sieve. Makes 3 cups.

Marinara Sauce

Salsa Marinara

1¼ cups extra-virgin olive oil

8 garlic cloves, crushed

1 35-ounce can peeled
San Marzano Italian plum
tomatoes, seeded and lightly
crushed, with their liquid

8 fresh basil leaves, julienned

Pinch of red pepper flakes

1 teaspoon minced fresh
Italian parsley

½ teaspoon dried oregano

1 teaspoon sugar

Salt and pepper

Heat the olive oil in a saucepan over medium heat until hot but not smoking. Add the garlic and cook until lightly brown, about 2 minutes; do not burn. Add the tomatoes and their liquid and bring to a boil. Season with salt and pepper to taste. Lower the heat and simmer, stirring frequently with a wooden spoon, for about 25 minutes. Add the basil, red pepper flakes, parsley, and oregano and cook another 8 minutes. Stir in the sugar. Strain the mixture through a colander set over a bowl. This sauce can be made a few days in advance and refrigerated. Makes approximately 4 cups.

Pesto Sauce

Salsa Pesto

2 cups fresh basil leaves, no stems (do not rinse the basil leaves; wipe them off with a paper towel)

2 garlic cloves, crushed

½ cup pine nuts

½ teaspoon freshly ground black pepper

½ cup extra-virgin olive oil

¼ cup freshly grated Pecorino cheese

1 tablespoon heavy cream

Salt

In a food processor or blender combine the basil, garlic, pine nuts, and pepper. Pulse to chop the mixture. With the machine running, gradually add the olive oil in a slow stream until blended. Stir in the cheese and cream and season with salt to taste. Makes approximately 1 cup.

Tomato Vinaigrette

Salsa Vinaigrette con Pomodoro

2 medium-size ripe tomatoes

¼ cup coarsely chopped mixed herbs, such as basil, marjoram, tarragon, and fennel

¼ cup fresh lemon juice

2 large shallots, peeled, coarsely chopped

1 cup extra-virgin olive oil

Put the tomatoes in boiling water for about 5 seconds; do not overcook or the tomatoes will turn to mush. Plunge the tomatoes immediately into an ice water bath for about 30 seconds. Peel off the skin and discard. Cut each in half and hold the tomato halves cut side down and squeeze out the seeds. Dice the tomatoes and put them in a sieve over a bowl to drain.

In a bowl mix all ingredients together. Then add the tomatoes and toss until mixed. Makes 1 cup.

Tomato Sauce

Salsa di Pomodoro

1 fresh ripe tomato

¼ cup extra-virgin olive oil, plus 2 tablespoons

½ cup minced onion

1 35–ounce can peeled San Marzano Italian plum tomatoes, seeded and lightly crushed, with their liquid

2 bay leaves

1 pinch red pepper flakes

4 carrot sticks and 4 celery ribs, tied into a bundle with butcher's string

1 garlic clove, crushed

1 tablespoon sugar

6 fresh basil leaves

Salt and pepper

Plunge the tomato in boiling water and cook until the skin begins to loosen, about 2 minutes (no longer). Place the tomato in ice water for a minute, then remove the skin. Using a fork to avoid handling the tomato too much, cut the tomato into quarters. Squeeze out the seeds.

Heat the olive oil in a saucepan over medium heat. Add the onions and cook, stirring frequently, until they are translucent, about 4 minutes. Add the canned tomatoes, bay leaves, red pepper flakes, and vegetable bundle. Season with salt and pepper to taste. Heat to boiling; reduce the heat to low and simmer, uncovered, for about 45 minutes, stirring frequently. Remove the vegetable bundle and bay leaves. Force the mixture through a food mill or strain through a colander set over a bowl and refrigerate the sauce for up to 2 or 3 days.

When you are ready to use the sauce, heat 2 tablespoons of olive oil in a saucepan until hot but not smoking. Sauté the crushed garlic clove until brown; remove the garlic. In the same pan, add the tomato sauce and cook until the sauce is warm, stirring occasionally with a wooden spoon. Add 1 tablespoon of sugar and 6 fresh basil leaves and stir well. Makes approximately 3 cups.

THREE

The Sixties in Germany, England, and the Bahamas

Learning the Restaurant Business

FERDIE: In Germany, not only did you have the Cold War going on, but the weather wasn't cooperating either. And what with cold weather, different food, a difficult language, and no friends, life there must have seemed unbearable. You've said that those minor inconveniences kept you speaking "survival" German and smiling a lot.

But at the restaurant Möevenpick all your hard work paid off. Soon you were moving up in the ranks. It must have felt good to purchase your first new car, an off-white four-door Ford Taurus.

NINO: It was a very proud moment for me. On my days off I kept cleaning the car, detailing it, putting antirust cream on all the chrome parts. I kept it so shiny that it looked like a mirror. I bought a nice red Grundig radio. I was at the height of my life in terms of freedom, and I started to manage my own finances and myself.

After a year there, I chose to work in another nice, old, peaceful, and serene city. I chose Hanover because of its rich history. But for me both the town and the people were too cold, and it never stopped snowing. It is said that the most well mannered people in Germany are from Hanover.

This was my first job with the InterContinental Hotel chain. I could never imagine that one day I would become the manager of one of its hotels. I was a waiter in the gourmet restaurant, Prinz Tavern. But I did not like it there, maybe because of the uniform I had to wear: short puffed pants to the knee and a white shirt with large puffed sleeves and a red *gilé* waistcoat. I felt like a Cossack, and it made me extremely self-conscious because of my bowlegs. To escape, I would often go to the forest, where the air was scented with wood smoke and what seemed to be roasting duck. I would sit under an old tree and listen to FM stations on my new radio. Back at home the family radio got only AM stations, so I loved listening to the wonderful FM music.

Nino in Hanover, 1966. Nino Pernetti collection.

I could not take the cold anymore so, after the harsh, cold winter, I decided to go south, to Bodensee [Lake Constance] and the Hotel Wilder Mann in Meersburg. It was the end of spring and I was happy to be back in the warm weather and to see the blue water again. The hotel restaurant was bustling. The lake sits 395 meters above sea level and is Europe's third largest. It touches three nations: Germany, Austria, and Switzerland. The weather is among the mildest and sunniest in Germany. The hotel was a very old one, and it was Meersburg's favorite.

Customers loved the hotel. The restaurant was situated in a rose garden with many types of roses. People came by to see them as if it were a rose museum. We would serve lunch, and the fragrance of roses and gardenias filled the air; it was magnificent. The best tables were those in the garden on the side of the cliff above the lake. Lunch was served daily from noon to 2:00 p.m. Patrons waited in line for their favorite table with the

Nino with his new car, Meersburg, 1967. Nino Pernetti collection.

Hotel Wilder Mann staff. Nino is in back row, fifth from right. Meersburg, 1967. Nino Pernetti collection.

best view. The atmosphere, the ambiance, with birds flying from tree to tree, was magical. After lunch, from 3:00 to 6:00 p.m., there was a tea dance with a live band. It was popular and attracted many tourists. We would serve Melitta coffee and a wide selection of petits fours and cakes from the pastry trolley. I loved to work there. When you have fun at what you do, everything is easy.

I met Carlo Cenni here. Carlo was from Florence and he was my busboy. We became good friends, and our friendship has lasted to this day, forty years later. Carlo did well for himself; now he is the general manager of Il Guelfo Bianco, a small boutique bed-and-breakfast hotel in the heart of Florence. I stay there when I visit Florence, and we reminisce about those days in Germany.

At the end of the summer season, in mid-September, I returned to the Möevenpick restaurant in Frankfurt as the bar manager. I had to pass a demanding exam on cocktails. Furthermore, I had to know the composition of the different liqueurs. Quite a few times I got tipsy trying each one in order to acquire the taste. The only thing I was not happy about was the approaching winter.

FERDIE: In mid-April 1968, after two and a half years in Germany, you decided it was time to move on to another country and you relocated to England. You were twenty-three years old. An employment agency found you a job in Moretonhampstead with a very prestigious hotel, the Manor House Hotel.

NINO: I took the train to Hoek van Holland from Frankfurt and embarked on the overnight ferry to England, continuing by train to Exeter in Devon. I arrived at 5:30 p.m., and the hotel's car was awaiting me. As we drove to the hotel, about an hour's ride over bumpy country roads, the driver asked me where I came from. I said Germany. My knowledge of English was poor so I answered his questions with a "yes" or a "no." After a few minutes the driver said, "You don't look German to me and more so because of your accent." He asked me again, "Where do you come from? Where were you born?"

Manor House Hotel in Moretonhampstead, 1968. Nino Pernetti collection.

"I am from Italy," I said proudly. The driver's face suddenly lit up with a big smile and he said, "Well, you will be happy to know that the head bartender is Italian, so is the maître d' and also a bunch of cooks and waiters." I hid my disappointment. The reason I had chosen a secluded place in England, and not a metropolitan city, was to avoid my fellow Italians, because I would then end up speaking Italian instead of learning English. But it was too late. The driver took me to Moretonhampstead, which is a little village in the heart of Devon. The Manor House Hotel was beautiful and picturesque, almost like a medieval castle, with a magnificent golf course amid small ponds, creeks, gazebos, and flowers of every color of the rainbow. It was mostly for rich old folks, staying 2–3 weeks at a time.

The waiters served in white gloves and black tie, very stiff and reserved. It was a pleasure to work there. And here was my stepping-stone to bigger things. England was an eye-opener for me because of the overabundance of everything. There was a new language to learn, people with a different mind-set than the continent (as they used to say), and they drove on the left side of the road.

There was great camaraderie between all the staff members; we were like the United Nations—all different nationalities. Since the hotel was in the middle of nowhere, the management provided staff quarters adjacent to the hotel. Here we had our recreational room with TV, pool table, Ping-Pong, vending machines, and so on, and our own tennis court. This is where I learned to

A party at the Manor House Hotel. Nino *(second from left)* with maître d' Mr. Rossi, Moretonhampstead, 1968. Nino Pernetti collection.

Nino *(left)* playing soccer in Exeter, 1968. Nino Pernetti collection.

play tennis and developed a great passion for it, second only to my passion for soccer. Some of us even pooled money to purchase an old 1950 car so on our days off we could explore the surrounding areas or go to the beach in Torbay. The closest town was Exeter, twenty-two miles away. There was only a single bus going there once a day. It would leave at 8:00 a.m. and come back at 4:00 p.m. On Sunday we played soccer against each other in miniformat teams.

The food in England was no better than the food in Germany, but here at least there was compensation; breakfast was a banquet with twenty kinds of cereals, stewed fruits, smoked haddock, and kippers. The Devonshire cream is the best in England. It is fresh, thick, and delicious. Scrambled eggs, bacon, sausages, along with the best orange marmalade and different fruit-flavored jams. They make the best marmalade in the world. I never saw a country where people read as many newspapers. Every patron would read the newspaper while waiting to be served breakfast.

With my broken English, I felt the need to take private lessons twice a week. Between my lunch and dinner breaks, I rode an old bicycle I had purchased for five pounds; on rainy days, more often than not, I drove "our" car to the home of a very nice elderly couple, Mr. and Mrs. Sullivan. Mr. Sullivan was a retired navy admiral in his late seventies, small, with a tiny mustache and short hair which looked to me like a toupee. He was very fatherly toward me.

Every afternoon his wife would prepare tea for us at 4:30 on the dot. It was served in their colorful living room, which was decorated in the style of Laura Ashley, and always with her finest china. Here is where I was taught the ritual of the preparation and drinking of tea, very ceremonial. She would heat the water in a teakettle then pour it into her fine china teapot, letting the tea stand for five minutes before she poured it into the cups. Then the milk was added to your taste. It was all new to me, and because I was accustomed to drinking tea with lemon, at first it tasted to me like *caffèlatte*. But then I learned to like it.

While I was conversing with Mr. Sullivan I always knew when 4:30 was approaching because the whiff of wonderfully fresh baked cookies floated through the small kitchen, and soon Mrs. Sullivan would appear with a tray. They were the best cookies I've ever eaten. This was also a part of my lesson. I very much enjoyed my time learning from this gracious couple.

One day Mr. Sullivan asked me if I liked mountain hiking. I said yes. The following week, on my day off, he picked me up at the staff entrance of the hotel at

Nino going to the Sullivans' house for English lessons, 1968. Nino Pernetti collection.

8:00 a.m. sharp. We walked for three hours and then we stopped for lunch. He had brought along a couple of sandwiches, and we sat by a stream, where we drank the water to wash down the sandwiches. We reached a bee farm where Mr. Sullivan knew the people who ran the farm. They handed us mesh veils and some gloves so we could approach the bees to see how they produced honey. He told me a story that to this day I don't know whether to believe. He said that the best honey was made by female bees mated with Italian male bees!

On Thursdays and Sundays the hotel showed old movies to the guests. The staff could watch as well from the small mezzanine of the theater room. This was fun and a nice break, and the best opportunity to meet the female staff members and prospective girlfriends. Every waiter looked forward to movie night and with good reason. The movies always started at 8:30 p.m. Movie night was usually sold out, and the hotel dining room bustled with early-bird diners, who would come around 6:30 p.m. so they could finish in time to go to the movie.

Not every customer was interested in the movie, so they would come at the usual dinner hour, which was about 7:00 p.m. to 8:00 p.m. Each guest was assigned a permanent table during their stay. One night an American couple, the Gordons, walked into the dining room about 8:30 p.m. and noticed that the room was almost empty. They asked me why. I told them about movie night and that everyone, including employees, went to the movie. Mr. Gordon politely asked me if I wanted to see the movie and if so he would place his order and I could put everything on the table. Even though I wanted to go badly (the film that night was *Roman Holiday* with Audrey Hepburn and Gregory Peck) I did not want to disappoint them. I had to do my job, and I had learned to be gracious to all customers. No matter what the situation, it is always the customer who comes first. Each time I went into the kitchen to pick up their food I was afraid that the cook would take revenge and poison it.

They finished dining around 10:00 p.m., by which time the movie was ending. The following day during breakfast Mr. Gordon told me that they would be returning to the United States and said, "Nino, if you're interested, I will recommend you to the general manager at the Cotton Bay Club in Eleuthera, Bahamas, where I'm a board member." Even though I thought Mr. Gordon was trying to be nice to me because he probably could tell that I was a bit upset about missing the movie, I responded with a polite "Yes, thank you."

During breakfast service the waiters began to tease me. They kept bragging about how wonderful the movie was and how many new female employees were there. This was typical behavior. But lucky is the one who laughs last because three weeks later I received a thick envelope postmarked "The Islands of the Bahamas." It was 11:30, shortly before lunch, and, with my heart beating fast and full of emotion, I opened the envelope in private. Inside was a letter from the general manager offering me the job as maître d' upon the recommendation of Mr. Gordon. In the letter were outlined all the conditions. All the necessary forms for the work visa were also included. I jumped for joy and ran to the staff dining room, holding the letter high in the air and saying, "This is the movie's next libretto." This was my time. This was my even-steven with my colleagues for teasing me. Three weeks later I boarded a BOAC plane in London headed for New York and then to Eleuthera on Pan Am.

FERDIE: It was November of 1968 and you were preparing for a star turn as maître d'. You had bought an extensive gentleman's wardrobe. You got off the plane in intense heat so none of the clothes would do! The entire wardrobe would never be unpacked. Eleuthera was just taking off as the top hideaway for the rich and famous.

NINO: That was the final destination at the time. True, I served Nixon, Juan Trippe, senators, CEOs, and all of their entourages. In Eleuthera, it was said, time stood still. Life was leisurely, and peace was a reality and not an illusion. On my off days I pedaled to the native villages to absorb the island's flavor. More important, my romance with Miami began. Some big shots staying at the club rented a special box in Miami to see a Dolphins football game and invited me to come along. Thinking football meant soccer, I accepted the invitation, but once we landed in Miami I realized that it was not a soccer game, and I told them that I had changed my mind and instead took a tour of Miami and the beach. I fell head over heels in love with Miami. I made up my mind that one day I would work and live there.

FERDIE: While you were now proficient in German, your English needed a bit more practice transitioning from a British to an American accent.

NINO: I would listen attentively as they talked to me on the phone, and I would always say, "Don't worry! Don't worry!" One day this got me in a gigantic bind. Our New Year's Eve party was going to be a blockbuster! It was totally sold out. In fact, it was overbooked, and I couldn't understand where all of these people were coming from, since there were more reservations than room in the club. The answer to the puzzle was that many customers had made double reservations; they were sharing the table with other people, and those people, too, had reserved, creating an unexpected overbooking. I was in total consternation, and I did not want to go to the general manager and explain my problem to him. After all, I was the maître d' and I was supposed to know what I was doing.

It was 11:00 a.m. New Year's Eve morning, and I was in a complete state of confusion. What do I do now? How do I fit in 30 percent more people than the club's capacity? An idea came to me when I overheard one of my captains, Leroy, asking a fellow worker if the fireworks were ready for tonight's celebration at their village. Immediately, my mind lit up and I thought, "Here is the solution."

First, I told Leroy that I wanted to buy these fireworks and put them on display outside the restaurant by the pool. He said, "Mr. Nino, they never have had this here before, and it is quite costly." I said, "Precisely," and with a firm voice I told him, "I must have these fireworks at any cost. If you succeed in this mission you will have a privileged position throughout my stay here; you have my word." I gave him $500 out of my own pocket and off he went. I called Hilbert, my assistant, gave him the house list, and said, "Go on the golf course, the club house, the beach, the Marina and ask each one if they want to sit outside on the terrace or inside the restaurant. Tell them there will be fireworks tonight. Write down their names and the names of each person in the party, and if you see a name already written down as being part of another party, ask for the first name so there will be no name confusion." Since we had forty seats on the terrace and ninety inside, I told him, "If you see that you are going above forty outside, stop offering the

Nino and Leroy, Cotton Bay Club, Eleuthera, 1968. Nino Pernetti collection.

terrace." I told him the same thing I told Leroy: succeed in this mission and you will be a star on my team.

I would be short two captains at lunch and I knew the service would suffer. I went to the kitchen and told the chef, Helmuth, that, because I was short two captains, we should have only half of the menu available. It would facilitate an easy service. I explained to the customers that, because of the preparations for the evening, we had a reduced lunch menu.

Lunch was over and neither captain was back yet. I started to learn about the pace of life in the Bahamas. Leroy arrived first, at 2:30 p.m. I could see his bright smile a mile away. I understood that he had succeeded, although the price for the fireworks was $750. By 4:00 p.m. I was frantic; no signs of Hilbert. I phoned the golf club, and they told me he had left fifty minutes earlier, so any minute he should show up. In the meantime, to add to the tension, I had the chef on my back because he wanted to know the final count. I tried to calm him down and told him just to start, but he was German and demanded precision. Me, being Italian, I was giving him charm and a smile—not the head count. Finally, the captain showed up with about ten pages in his hand. After thoroughly studying the list I came in with the final count, which was in line with the number of people staying in the club. Thus we averted disaster and made people happy, including the chef, who still wanted a precise number. What a relief.

Now the eternal headache of a restaurant: Who gets the best table? I put this aside for the moment. I told the staff to start to prepare according to the plan I had made. While they were setting the tables up I went to see the general manager. Mr. Pfeiffer did not want deviations from rules and regulations. I informed him about the fireworks. When I said fireworks he said a quick and firm "no," that it was too dangerous and they had never had fireworks in the history of the club. I thought to myself, "How am I going to tell him that everyone already knows and is expecting fireworks?" I had a big problem on my hands. I waited a few seconds, took a deep breath, and stretched the truth a bit: "This idea was from Mr. Trippe's grandson John." Mr. Pfeiffer understood right away and said, "Well, if this is the case, then let's go ahead, but coordinate with the chief engineer for the location and safety."

I ran out of his office ecstatic. At once I went to look for John and when I found him I explained my situation. He said, "No problem, Nino. The fireworks were my idea." John and I played tennis every afternoon so we were good friends.

The celebration was a success. But not everything ran smoothly that evening. Mr. Charles Eaves, the chairman of Goodyear Tires, had as his guests the Nixons, Richard and Donald, and Nixon's friend Bebe Rebozo, with their wives. At the last minute he called and ordered a table for ten. In my poor English I said, "Don't worry! Don't worry!" I thought he meant New Year's Day, and we had plenty of room for that day.

Imagine my shock when Mr. Eaves showed up on New Year's Eve with the Nixons and Bebe Rebozo in tow! He wanted the reserved table for ten now, and every table in the house was sold. I invited them to have a cocktail at the bar while I made arrangements to get them set up. I added another row of tables at the edge of the dance floor because I figured that elderly people would not want to dance. It was a close call. But that was not the end of my exciting New Year's.

Serving Richard Nixon and Bebe Rebozo at a later date in Key Biscayne, 1985. Nino Pernetti collection.

For New Year's Day Mr. Trippe wanted a special brunch-buffet set up for him and his twenty guests on the restaurant's terrace. No expense was to be spared, so the buffet was decorated with ice sculptures. The buffet included sumptuous lobster medallions, a fountain of shrimp, fois gras, and beef tenderloins in aspic. I put the best waiters around the buffet table. There was a flash fire in the kitchen as the buffet was being set up, and I called all the staff to rush to the kitchen to help take care of the mess.

While the staff was in the kitchen, some of the club's guests arrived at the restaurant and thought the buffet was for them. When I returned from the kitchen, the buffet was a wreck; to make matters worse, there was no more lobster or shrimp available on the entire island.

I received a call from the marina manager that Mr. Trippe's yacht had just arrived and was being anchored. I summoned the chef and quickly instructed him to fill the buffet with tropical fruits as best he could while I ran to the marina to greet Mr. Trippe and his guests to give the chef more time to replenish the buffet. Every minute counted. The first to step down was Fred Astaire followed by Rudolf Nureyev. All the ceremonial introductions and New Year's wishes gave us enough time for Chef Helmuth to finish the buffet. I looked at my watch and realized that Mr. Trippe was running an hour and a half late, so I informed him that I had had to remove the seafood from the buffet as a safety measure and he nodded in agreement.

Rudolf Nureyev. Ferdie and Luisita Pacheco collection.

Though the island was a glamorous resort, for me and for the rest of the expatriate employees it was boring. There was nothing to do—no radio, no movies, and we could not mix with club members. There was only sun and the beaches. I was the only privileged one because I had contact with customers, and once in a while they took me on a fishing trip.

I soon realized that fishing was not my cup of tea. My enthusiasm for my job kept me going, but I missed Europe, playing soccer, and eating good pasta. I played tennis with Mr. Trippe's grandchildren when they came down from New York and I played tennis with the president of the club's holding company, Mr. Newman, who was in his sixties. Mr. Newman had a cottage on the premises and would knock on my door Sunday morning at 6:00 a.m., which was far too early for me. He wanted to play that early because in late morning and the afternoons it was too hot. We always had a bet: if he won, I had to help him clean, wash, and polish his single-engine Cessna; if I won, he had to fly me around the island. Honestly, I did not like to fly with him because he flew so low at times that I could see sharks and stingrays. It scared me to death. Though Mr. Newman played tennis better than me, I was younger and had speed on my side, so the matches were about even.

Nino playing tennis in Eleuthera, 1969. Nino Pernetti collection.

The Bahamas was a great learning experience for me. I changed the restaurant's concept. Gone were the perennial shrimp cocktail, steak, and baked potato. I introduced nice Italian and French specialties and the flaming-dessert cart. At any given moment you could see waiters preparing flaming desserts among the tables, which was a nice touch of color for the people who had spent all day on the golf course or on the boat.

Before dinner everyone congregated at the Windjammer Bar for martinis. I would go there and stroll among them, shaking hands, kissing the ladies, asking how their game went. I would tell them about the day's specials. One day Mr. Trippe spoke about "my hotels." He told me that he wanted me to work in one of his hotels, and, not knowing what he meant, I said, "Yes, no problem."

On a Friday in May 1969, Juan Trippe, the hard-

Buffet setup at the Cotton Bay Club, Eleuthera, 1969. Nino Pernetti collection.

hitting CEO of Pan American Airlines, changed the course of my career. He called me to his cottage and said he had good news for me. "Nino, this airline ticket is for you to go to New York on Monday. Take a taxi to the Pan Am Building, offices of the InterContinental Hotels. Go to the eighty-ninth floor; they will be waiting for you."

At first I did not make the connection. I had worked for InterContinental Hotels in Hanover, but I did not know that InterContinental Hotels was a major U.S. hotel chain at that time. With some hesitation, I went to Mr. Pfeiffer's office to give him the news, but he had already spoken to Mr. Trippe and said he was very happy for me. He shook my hand and wished me luck. I was to fly to New York the next day. As I left for the New York offices, I thought that I had reached the pinnacle; I was at the top of my field. Or was I?

Everything was overwhelming—the skyscrapers, the crowds, the pushing, the shoving, the electricity, the taxis, the wheeling and dealing. Once in New York, I was so impressed that I decided to walk to the Pan Am Building instead of taking a taxi. Since the meeting was in the afternoon I had time. I had never been in New

York. I visited the Empire State Building, bought five tickets to send to my family in Italy as proof of my being there. I spent the morning walking all over New York City and taking it all in. I walked the streets until time for the meeting at 3:00 p.m. The doorman at the Pan Am Building made a phone call and then guided me to the elevators, which took me to the eighty-ninth floor.

In 1969 I was not yet fluent in English but I spoke slowly and carefully. I did not want to embarrass Mr. Trippe, who had recommended me, and I was also a bit nervous. While waiting in the reception room I stood by the Italian American receptionist and flirted a little because I wanted to be nice to everyone.

Mr. Wassey, the personnel manager, told me that I would be going to the InterContinental Hotel in Managua, Nicaragua, as the maître d' for the rooftop restaurant. But first I had to return to the Bahamas for a month until a replacement could be found, and I was allowed to go home to Italy for a couple of weeks of rest and relaxation before flying to Nicaragua. I socialized with my friends in Salò and while there made my travel arrangements.

While in Italy I received a telegram from New York to call Mr. Wassey urgently. I was worried because I thought they had changed their minds. The telegram read: "Change of plans. You are to go to Kabul, Afghanistan. You have to report by next week to Mr. Pierre Martinet, General Manager. Proceed changing your tickets and airline reservation."

The hotel in Kabul was still under construction, but there was a lot of training to do with the local staff. The general manager needed me there quickly. I was convinced I was going to Africa. I was so awestruck that I did not make the clear connection between Kabul and Afghanistan. I just thought, "Africa, how wonderful!"

The day before my departure for Kabul I was driven to the Milan airport by my brother Bruno and my father. As I was checking in at the Alitalia ticket counter, I realized that I had left the bag containing my passport and other valuable papers in my brother's car. I told the ticket counter attendant that I would be back shortly and I ran quickly to see if my brother was still there, but he had already sped away toward Salò. Panic overtook me, but, fortunately, the flight to Kabul was not leaving until the following day out of Rome.

I decided to take the bus from the airport to downtown Milan, where Bruno shared an apartment with a friend, Serafino. But when I got there, Bruno had not arrived. He had gone to Salò to drop off my father. I then asked Serafino whether he could drive me to Salò to get my bag from Bruno's car. I left my brother a note stating that I drove to Salò with Serafino to recover my bag and that I would be back to sleep at the apartment.

It was a two-hour drive from Milan. We left late in the afternoon and arrived at 8:00 p.m. Everyone was surprised to see us. Bruno had gone back to Milan and had left my bag in Salò. After explanations and a quick dinner prepared by my mother, we were off again to Milan, where I was to spend the night at my brother's apartment then take an early flight from Milan to Rome en route to Kabul.

Serafino had just purchased a Fiat 850 and had just gotten his driver's license, so he was driving quite slowly. Ten minutes into the trip back to Milan I asked him to let me drive, since I was a more experienced driver and more familiar with the roads. It was late and I had been up for almost eighteen hours, so the inevitable happened. I fell asleep and rammed the car into a concrete highway divider. Serafino broke both legs and I flew through the windshield. No seat belts in those days. A good Samaritan called an ambulance and took us to Brescia's main hospital. There the nurse bandaged my bloodied head, elbows, and knees and took X-rays. While she prepared me for bed she asked where I was from. "I'm from Salò but I was originally born in Campione at Lake Garda."

"Oh, I have some relatives there," said the nurse.

Sensing that this nurse was kind, I told her about my predicament: "You know I have work in Africa and I must catch my flight tomorrow in Rome. If I don't make it I will lose my job. What can I do?"

"Well, if you feel good tomorrow and if you are over twenty-one you sign some papers and they can release you. You are very lucky that you have no broken bones,

Nino with friends in hotel school, Gardone, Riviera, 1964. Nino Pernetti collection.

just cuts and bruises. You tell the doctor so he can release you."

My brother Bruno was frantic with worry; it was 2:00 a.m. and still no word from us. Bruno called all the hospitals and clinics around Milan, the police stations, too. Finally, he found out where we were.

Early the next morning a few patients were standing around my bed staring at me; their voices woke me up. Both of my elbows were bandaged, so I could not touch my injured head. I asked one of them if he could touch my "turban" made of bandages. They thought I was delirious and called for the doctor. I told him about my situation and, after a checkup, he released me. I got dressed and looked for Serafino. I told him that I was sorry for what had happened and that I would take care of his car, hospital expenses, and his lost time from work. I took a taxi to the Milan airport—it cost me a fortune—no time for the bus or train.

When Bruno got to the hospital in Brescia, he was told that I had been released on my own accord. Bruno found Serafino, who informed him of what had happened.

When you are young, the fear of losing your job is the main concern in your life. I had strong recommendations but, in my mind, if I didn't arrive on time, I would lose my job. For me the job was everything.

I arrived at the airport in Rome, took the ticket out of my shirt pocket, put it on the counter of Ariana Airways. While the attendant was checking me in I looked up and saw on the wall a huge map with dotted lines showing the flight's route. At first I did not see Kabul. Then the route's unbending trajectory from Athens, to Bombay, and then Kabul hit me like a ton of bricks! All I could say was, "Please give me back my ticket. I am going to Africa."

"But your ticket is to Kabul, Afghanistan," said the agent. I just had to ask as a sort of reality check, "Where is Afghanistan?" By now the very nice young woman was staring at me in disbelief: "Afghanistan is not in Africa!"

So I went to Afghanistan.

PASTA

Farfalle with Chicken Livers and Broccoli

Farfalle con Fegatini di Pollo e Broccoli

4 tablespoons unsalted butter

1 large onion, minced

1½ cups chopped chicken livers

½ teaspoon cayenne pepper

2 tablespoons coarse salt

1 pound premium Italian farfalle

3 cups fresh broccoli florets

2 tablespoons extra-virgin olive oil

Salt and pepper

Start cooking the pasta 5 minutes before you start the sauce.

In a large pot bring 6 quarts of water to a full boil. Add the 2 tablespoons of coarse salt and gradually add the farfalle. Cook for 10 minutes, stirring frequently. After 4 minutes, add the broccoli. Drain the pasta and broccoli and return them to the pot. While the pasta is cooking, heat butter in a large skillet over medium-high heat; add the onion and sauté until golden. Add the chicken livers and cook for 3 minutes, stirring constantly. Season with salt and pepper to taste and the cayenne pepper. Keep warm.

Combine the chicken livers and olive oil with the pasta. Transfer to warm plates. Serves 4.

Wine pairings: Poggio Antico Rosso di Montalcino; Rodney Strong Pinot Noir.

Fettuccine with Two Prosciuttos

Fettuccine ai Due Prosciutti

2 tablespoons coarse salt

1 pound premium Italian fettuccine

2 egg yolks

1¼ cup heavy cream

1 teaspoon hot paprika

2 slices Italian prosciutto, cut into strips

2 slices Italian boiled prosciutto, cut into strips

½ cup freshly grated Parmesan cheese, plus more for garnish

Salt and pepper

Start cooking the pasta 5 minutes before you start the sauce.

In a large pot bring 6 quarts of water to a full boil. Add the 2 tablespoons of coarse salt. Gradually add the pasta and cook for 7 minutes, stirring frequently. Drain the pasta and return it to the pot.

While the pasta is cooking, heat the egg yolks and cream in a small pan over low heat, whisking continuously. Season with salt and pepper to taste and the paprika. The sauce should thicken slightly but never boil. Add both prosciuttos and cook over low heat for 3 minutes. Toss the sauce with the pasta 3–4 times. Add the ½ cup Parmesan cheese and toss again. Divide evenly among 4 warmed plates. Toss and serve with grated Parmesan cheese. Serves 4.

Wine pairings: Pieropan Classico Superiore; Chateau St. Jean Fumé Blanc.

Fettuccine with Boiled Prosciutto

Fettuccine con Prosciutto Cotto

2 tablespoons coarse salt

1 pound premium Italian fettuccine

2 tablespoons unsalted butter, divided

¼ cup extra-virgin olive oil, divided

1 medium onion, minced

4 medium carrots, shaved into ribbons with a vegetable peeler

6 ounces thickly sliced Italian boiled Prosciutto, cut into thin strips

¼ cup dry white wine

½ teaspoon grated nutmeg

½ cup chicken stock

¼ cup freshly grated Parmesan cheese

Salt and pepper

Start to cook the pasta 5 minutes before you start the sauce.

In a large pot bring 6 quarts of water to a boil. Add the two tablespoons of coarse salt. Gradually add the pasta and cook for 7 minutes, stirring frequently. Drain the pasta and return it to the pot.

While the pasta is cooking, in a large skillet heat 1 table-spoon of the butter and 2 tablespoons of the olive oil over moderately high heat until hot but not smoking. Add the onion and cook, stirring, until translucent, 2–3 minutes. Add the carrots, prosciutto, and wine and cook until the prosciutto changes color, 8–10 minutes. Add the nutmeg, then the chicken stock and simmer for 4–5 minutes. Season with salt and pepper to taste.

Toss the remaining butter and oil and the Parmesan cheese with the pasta, then add the prosciutto mix-ture and toss again a few times. Divide evenly among 4 warmed plates. Serves 4.

Wine pairings: Bertani Valpolicella Secco; Columbia Estates Merlot.

see color plate 9

Fusilli with Eggplant

Fusilli con Melanzane

2 tablespoons coarse salt

1 pound premium Italian fusilli

2 medium eggplants, peeled, sliced ½-inch thick, then diced

6 tablespoons extra-virgin olive oil, divided, plus extra for drizzling

½ cup minced onions

2 cloves garlic, minced

½ tablespoon dried oregano

¼ cup dry white wine

½ cup freshly grated Parmesan cheese, plus extra for garnish

3 tablespoons minced Italian parsley

Salt and pepper

Start to cook the pasta 6 minutes before you start the sauce.

Sprinkle the eggplant with salt and drain in a colander for 35 minutes to release excess water, stirring from time to time. Pat the eggplant dry with paper towels.

In a large pot bring 6 quarts of water to a full boil. Add the 2 tablespoons of coarse salt. Gradually add the pasta and cook for 8 minutes, stirring frequently. Drain the pasta and return it to the pot.

While the pasta is cooking, heat 3 tablespoons olive oil in a sauté pan until hot but not smoking and brown the eggplant and onion. Season with salt and pepper to taste and add the garlic, oregano, and wine. Cook for about 16 minutes, or until the eggplant is tender.

Toss the eggplant mixture and the remaining olive oil with the pasta 3–4 times. Add the ½ cup Parmesan cheese and toss again 3–4 times. Divide evenly among 4 warmed plates. Garnish with minced parsley and drizzle with olive oil. Serves 4.

Wine pairings: Libaio Ruffino Chardonnay; Simi Chardonnay.

see color plate 10

Fusilli with Italian Sausage

Fusilli con Salsiccie

2 tablespoons coarse salt

1 pound premium Italian fusilli

2 tablespoons extra-virgin olive oil

1 pound Italian sausage, sliced

1 medium onion, sliced

½ red bell pepper, cut into strips

½ cup Cabernet

½ cup shredded fresh basil leaves

½ cup freshly grated Parmesan cheese

8 fresh basil leaves, for garnish

Salt and pepper

Start cooking the pasta 5 minutes before you start the sauce.

In a large pot bring 6 quarts of water to a full boil. Add the 2 tablespoons of coarse salt. Gradually add the pasta and cook for 8 minutes, stirring frequently. Drain the pasta and return it to the pot.

While the pasta is cooking, heat the olive oil in a large skillet over medium-high heat until hot but not smoking. Brown the sausage, stirring with a wooden spoon, 10–12 minutes. Using a slotted spoon, transfer the sausage to a bowl.

Add the onion to the skillet and sauté until golden brown. Add the bell pepper and cook 5–6 minutes. Add the Cabernet and cook another 5 minutes to allow the wine to evaporate partially. Season with salt and pepper to taste. Combine the onion mixture, the sausage, and the shredded basil.

Add the onion and sausage mixture to the pasta and toss 3–4 times with a large spoon. Add the Parmesan cheese and toss again. Divide evenly among 4 warmed plates and garnish each with 2 basil leaves. Serves 4.

Wine pairings: Fassati Selciaia Rosso di Montepulciano; Francis Coppola Claret.

see color plate 11

Fusilli with Ricotta

Fusilli con Ricotta

2 tablespoons coarse salt

1 pound premium Italian fusilli

1 cup fresh ricotta (about ½ pound)

1 garlic clove, crushed

1 tablespoon chopped oil-packed sun-dried tomatoes (reserve 1 teaspoon oil)

2 tablespoons fresh basil chopped

3 tablespoons extra-virgin olive oil, divided

2 pounds tomatoes, seeded and chopped

2 tablespoons freshly grated Parmesan cheese

½ tablespoon minced Italian parsley

Salt and pepper

In a large pot bring 6 quarts water to a boil. Add the 2 tablespoons of coarse salt. Gradually add the pasta and cook for 8 minutes, stirring frequently. Drain the pasta and return it to the pot.

While the pasta is cooking, in a mini food processor, combine the ricotta with the basil, the garlic, the sun-dried tomatoes, 1 teaspoon oil, and 1 tablespoon of the olive oil. Season with salt and pepper to taste and purée until smooth.

In a large bowl, toss the tomatoes with the remaining 2 tablespoons of olive oil; season with salt and pepper to taste. Toss the ricotta mixture with the pasta a few times. Add the Parmesan cheese and toss 3–4 times. Divide evenly among 4 warmed plates and sprinkle each plate with parsley. Serves 4.

Wine pairings: Livio Felluga or Pinot Grigio; Robert Mondavi Fumé Blanc.

see color plate 12

Linguine with Clams

Linguine alle Vongole

50 fresh littleneck clams

2 tablespoons coarse salt

1 pound premium Italian linguine

½ cup extra-virgin olive oil

5 cloves garlic, sliced

4 bay leaves

½ cup dry white wine

½ cup clam juice

½ cup fish stock

½ teaspoon crushed hot red pepper flakes

¼ cup minced fresh Italian parsley, divided

Salt and pepper

Place the clams in a large bowl of cold water and swirl them to clean the shells. With a hard brush, scrub the shells, including the joints. Place the cleaned clams in a colander and rinse them under cold water. Drain thoroughly.

Start to cook the pasta 5 minutes before you start the sauce. In a large pot bring 6 quarts of water to a boil. Add the 2 tablespoons of coarse salt. Gradually add the pasta and cook for 8 minutes, stirring frequently. Drain the pasta and return it to the pot.

While the pasta is cooking, heat the oil in a large skillet over medium-high heat until hot but not smoking. Scatter the garlic in the oil and cook until golden, about 2 minutes. Place the clams and bay leaves in the skillet and splash the wine, clam juice, and fish stock over them. Add the red pepper flakes and bring to a boil; lower the heat and cook until the clams have opened, about 10 minutes. Discard any unopened clams.

Add the pasta to the skillet and toss until well mixed. Bring the pasta and the sauce to a boil, stir in half of the parsley, and season with salt and pepper to taste. Divide the pasta and clams evenly among 4 warmed plates. Sprinkle each plate with the remaining chopped parsley. Serves 4.

Wine pairings: Santa Margherita Pinot Grigio; Chimney Rock Fumé Blanc.

Linguine with Shrimp

Linguine con Gamberi

1 cup fresh bread crumbs

3 tablespoons extra-virgin olive oil, divided

2 tablespoons minced black Italian Gaeta olives

2 tablespoons chopped oil-packed sun-dried tomatoes, 1 tablespoon oil reserved

1 tablespoon Modena balsamic vinegar

2 tablespoons coarse salt

1 pound premium Italian linguine

1 pound small shrimp, peeled and deveined

¾ cup dry white wine

1 cup finely chopped ripe tomatoes

2 tablespoons minced Italian parsley

½ cup shredded Pecorino cheese

Salt and pepper

Preheat the oven to 400°F.

On a baking sheet, toss the bread crumbs with 1 tablespoon of the olive oil and season with salt and pepper to taste. Bake for 12 minutes.

In a bowl, combine the olives, sun-dried tomatoes, balsamic vinegar, 1 tablespoon of the olive oil, and the reserved oil from the tomatoes.

Start to cook the pasta 5 minutes before you start the sauce. In a large pot bring 6 quarts of water to a full boil. Add the 2 tablespoons of coarse salt. Gradually add the pasta and cook for 8 minutes, stirring frequently. Drain the pasta and return it to the pot.

In a large skillet, heat the remaining tablespoon of olive oil until simmering. Season the shrimp with salt and pepper to taste and add to the skillet. Cook over high heat about 2 minutes on each side. Transfer the shrimp to a bowl and keep them warm. Add the wine to the skillet and cook, scraping up any browned bits, until reduced to ¼ cup, about 3 minutes. Add any accumulated juices from the shrimp and remove the pan from the heat.

In a bowl toss the tomatoes with the parsley and season with salt and pepper to taste.

Add the wine sauce, the olive mixture, and the tomatoes to the pasta, season with salt and pepper again, and toss 3–4 times. Arrange the shrimp on the pasta. Scatter the Pecorino cheese and bread crumbs over the pasta. Divide evenly among 4 warmed plates. Serves 4.

Wine pairings: Pieropan or Veneto Soave or Classico Superiore; Gregich Hills Fumé Blanc.

see color plate 13

Orecchiette with Broccoli Rabe

Orecchiette con Rapini

2 tablespoons coarse salt

2 pounds broccoli rabe, trimmed and stalks cut crosswise into 3-inch pieces

1 pound premium Italian orecchiette

2 tablespoons extra-virgin olive oil, divided

3 garlic cloves, sliced

½ teaspoon red pepper flakes

6 oil-packed anchovies, drained

¾ cup chicken stock

½ cup freshly grated Parmesan cheese

Salt and pepper

In a large pot bring 6 quarts of water to a full boil. Add the 2 tablespoons of coarse salt and the broccoli rabe and cook for 3 minutes. Using a slotted spoon transfer the broccoli rabe to a large bowl and cool. Keep the water at a boil and set aside ½ cup of the broccoli water.

Start to cook the pasta 5 minutes before you start the sauce. Gradually add the pasta to the boiling broccoli rabe water and cook for 10 minutes, stirring frequently. Drain the pasta and return it to the pot.

While the pasta is cooking, heat 1½ tablespoons olive oil in a large skillet over medium-high heat until hot but not smoking. Add the garlic and red pepper and cook, stirring constantly, until the garlic is golden, about 2 minutes. Add the anchovies and with a fork mash them into the oil until smooth, about 2 minutes. Add the chicken stock and scrape up any browned bits from the bottom of the pan. Cook until the stock is reduced by ⅔, about 5–7 minutes. Return the broccoli rabe to the pan and cook until heated through, about 1 minute.

Add the broccoli rabe mixture and the remaining half tablespoonful of oil to the pasta. Toss 3–4 times. If the pasta is too dry, add ½ cup of broccoli cooking water to moisten it. Divide evenly among 4 warmed plates, sprinkle with Parmesan cheese, and serve. Serves 4.

Wine pairings: Caputo Greco di Tufo; Ferrari Carano Fumé Blanc.

see color plate 14

Penne with Anchovies, Black Olives, and Capers

Penne Puttanesca

2 tablespoons coarse salt

1 pound premium Italian
penne

1 35-ounce can Italian plum
tomatoes, with liquid

¼ cup extra-virgin olive oil,
plus extra for drizzling

6 cloves garlic, crushed

6 oil-packed anchovy fillets,
coarsely chopped

1 teaspoon red pepper flakes

3 tablespoons black Italian
Gaeta olives, pitted and
quartered

¼ cup dry white wine

5 fresh basil leaves, shredded

2 tablespoons marinara sauce
(see recipe, page 59)

4 tablespoons capers

½ cup freshly grated
Parmesan cheese

4 tablespoons minced fresh
Italian parsley

Salt and pepper

Start to cook the pasta 5 minutes before you start the
sauce.

In a large pot bring 6 quarts of water to a full boil. Add the
2 tablespoons of coarse salt. Gradually add the pasta and
cook for 10 minutes, stirring frequently. Drain the pasta
and return it to the pot.

Pour the tomatoes and their liquid into a bowl. Mash
them with a wire whisk until crushed and set aside.

Heat ¼ cup olive oil in a large skillet over medium-high
heat until hot but not smoking. Add the garlic and cook
until lightly browned, about 2 minutes. Add the anchovies and, using a fork, mash them into the oil until
smooth. Add the red pepper flakes and olives and cook
over medium heat for 2 minutes. Add the wine, basil,
marinara sauce, capers, and tomatoes with their juices.
Simmer uncovered over medium heat for 10 minutes,
stirring constantly. Season with salt and pepper to taste.
Add the sauce to the pasta and toss a few times. Add
the Parmesan cheese and toss again a few times. Divide
evenly among 4 warmed plates. Sprinkle each plate with
parsley and drizzle with olive oil. Serves 4.

Wine pairings: Caputo Greco di Tufo; Sterling Vintner's Collection
Sauvignon Blanc.

Penne with Broccoli and Porcini Mushrooms

Penne con Broccoli e Porcini

½ pound dried porcini mushrooms

2 tablespoons coarse salt

1 pound premium Italian penne

1 tablespoon vegetable oil

3 tablespoons unsalted butter, divided

1 garlic clove, minced

1 large head broccoli cut into florets

2 tablespoons dry white wine

2 tablespoons chicken stock

2 tablespoons extra-virgin olive oil

2 garlic cloves, crushed

½ cup freshly grated Parmesan cheese

½ tablespoon minced Italian parsley

Salt and pepper

Soak the porcini mushrooms for 2 hours in tap water. Drain, reserving 2 tablespoons of the soaking liquid.

Start to cook the pasta 5 minutes before you start the sauce. In a large pot bring 6 quarts of water to a full boil. Add the 2 tablespoons of coarse salt. Gradually add the pasta and cook for 10 minutes, stirring frequently. Drain the pasta and return it to the pot, reserving 1 cup of cooking water.

Heat the vegetable oil and 2 tablespoons of the butter in a large skillet until hot but not smoking. Add the minced garlic and reduce the heat to medium. Cook the garlic, stirring frequently, until it turns pale golden. Add the broccoli and salt to taste and coat well with the oil. Add the wine and chicken stock and cook for 2 minutes; remove the pan from the heat.

Heat the olive oil in a large skillet over medium-high heat until hot but not smoking. Add the 2 crushed garlic cloves. When the garlic begins to turn golden, add the drained porcini mushrooms and cook for 2 minutes. Season with salt and pepper to taste and simmer a few minutes on low heat. Stir in the broccoli mixture. Raise the heat to high, stir in the pasta, Parmesan cheese, remaining butter, and the 2 tablespoons of reserved porcini soaking liquid. Should the pasta be too dry, add some of the reserved pasta-cooking water and toss 3–4 times. Divide the pasta evenly among 4 warmed plates. Sprinkle each plate with parsley. Serves 4.

Wine pairings: Pieropan Soave Classico Superiore; Robert Mondavi Fumé Blanc.

see color plate 15

Penne with Pancetta and Saffron

Penne con Pancetta e Zafferano

2 tablespoons coarse salt

1 pound premium Italian penne

2 tablespoons extra-virgin olive oil

¼ cup minced Italian pancetta

¼ medium onion, finely chopped

1 cup whipping cream

1 teaspoon strands of saffron

¼ teaspoon ground nutmeg

½ cup freshly grated Parmesan cheese

½ cup freshly shredded Pecorino cheese

Salt and pepper

Start to cook the pasta 5 minutes before you start the sauce.

In a large pot bring 6 quarts of water to a full boil. Add the 2 tablespoons of coarse salt. Gradually add the pasta and cook for 10 minutes, stirring frequently.

While the pasta is cooking, heat the olive oil in a large skillet over medium-high heat until hot but not smoking. Add the pancetta and cook for 2–3 minutes, stirring occasionally; do not allow it to crisp. Add the onion and cook until translucent, being careful not to burn. Add the cream and stir constantly with a wooden spoon for 3 minutes. Add the saffron and nutmeg and stir for 2 minutes. Season with salt and pepper to taste.

Drain the pasta and return to the pot. Pour the pancetta sauce into the pasta pot and toss 3–4 times. Add the Parmesan and toss 3–4 times. Divide the pasta evenly among 4 warmed plates. Top each plate with shredded Pecorino cheese. Serves 4.

Wine pairings: Santa Margherita, Pinot Grigio or Beringer Chardonnay.

see color plate 16

Penne with Pumpkin and Yogurt

Penne con Zucca e Yogurt

2 tablespoon coarse salt

15 ounces fresh pumpkin chunks

2 6-ounce cartons plain yogurt

1 pound premium Italian penne

⅔ cup shredded Pecorino cheese

Salt and pepper

In a large pot bring 6 quarts of water to a full boil. Add the 2 tablespoons of coarse salt. Add the pumpkin and cook for 5 minutes. Using a slotted spoon remove the pumpkin; cool it in cold water. Maintain the cooking water at a simmer on low heat for the pasta. Dice the pumpkin and force it through a mesh strainer with a wooden spoon. Combine the yogurt and the pumpkin purée well. Season with salt and pepper to taste.

Return the water to a boil. Add the pasta gradually and cook for 10 minutes, stirring frequently. Drain the pasta and return it to the pot. Toss the pumpkin mixture with the pasta 3–4 times. Divide the pasta evenly among 4 warmed plates and top with the Pecorino cheese. Serves 4.

Wine pairings: Caputo Grego di Tufo; Ferrari Carano Fumé Blanc.

see color plate 17

Spaghetti Carbonara

Spaghetti alla Carbonara

2 tablespoons coarse salt

1 pound premium Italian spaghetti

3 tablespoons extra-virgin olive oil

1 clove garlic, lightly crushed

¼ cup diced Italian pancetta

2 tablespoons dry white wine

3 eggs

2 egg yolks

½ cup freshly grated Parmesan cheese

⅓ cup freshly grated Pecorino cheese

½ tablespoon minced fresh lemon zest

1½ cup whipping cream

2 tablespoons Italian parsley, minced

Pepper

Start cooking the pasta 5 minutes before you start the sauce.

In a large pot bring 6 quarts of water to a full boil. Add the 2 tablespoons of coarse salt. Gradually add the pasta and cook for 8 minutes, stirring frequently. Drain the pasta.

While the pasta is cooking, heat the olive oil in a large skillet over medium-high heat until hot but not smoking. Sauté the garlic until golden; remove it with a slotted spoon and discard. Add the pancetta to the skillet and cook for 2–3 minutes, stirring occasionally; do not allow it to crisp. Add the wine and simmer until it evaporates, about 1 minute. Remove the pan from the heat and set aside to cool.

In a large mixing bowl lightly beat the eggs and egg yolks. Add the Parmesan and Pecorino, lemon zest, cream, and parsley. Season with pepper to taste. When the oil and the pancetta have cooled sufficiently not to cook the eggs, stir the eggs into the cheese mixture and transfer the mixture to a large skillet. Add the pasta and cook over medium-low heat until the mixture coats the spaghetti thickly, about 2 minutes. Toss a few times and divide evenly among 4 warmed plates. Serves 4.

Wine pairings: Santa Margherita Pinot Grigio; Mer Soleil Chardonnay.

Spaghetti with Fennel and Tomatoes

Spaghetti con Finocchi e Pomodori

2 tablespoons coarse salt

1 pound premium Italian spaghetti

1 medium yellow onion, thinly sliced

3 garlic cloves, crushed

2 large fennel bulbs, halved, cored, and thinly sliced crosswise

½ teaspoon fennel seeds, crushed

¼ cup extra-virgin olive oil

1 28-ounce can San Marzano peeled tomatoes, drained and lightly crushed

¼ cup freshly grated Parmesan cheese

Salt and pepper

Start cooking the pasta 5 minutes before you start the sauce.

In a large pot bring 6 quarts of water to a full boil. Add the 2 tablespoons of coarse salt. Gradually add the pasta and cook for 8 minutes, stirring frequently. Drain the pasta and return to the pot.

Preheat the oven to 350°F. In a roasting pan, combine the onion, garlic, fennel, and fennel seeds. Sprinkle with the olive oil and season with salt and pepper to taste. Bake for 25 minutes, stirring occasionally, until the fennel slices are tender when pierced with a knife. Remove the pan from the oven, add the tomatoes, and bake 15 minutes. Season with salt and pepper to taste.

Toss the fennel-tomato mixture with the pasta 3–4 times. Add the Parmesan cheese and toss again. Divide the pasta evenly among 4 warmed plates. Serves 4.

Wine pairings: Santa Margherita, Pinot Grigio, or Sterling Chardonnay.

Spaghetti with Shellfish

Spaghetti con Crostacei

12 fresh littleneck clams

12 fresh plum mussels

2 tablespoons coarse salt

1 pound premium Italian spaghetti

¼ cup extra-virgin olive oil

2 cloves garlic, thinly sliced

½ teaspoon red pepper flakes

8 medium shrimp, peeled and deveined

8 large langostinos, tail only

¼ cup dry Marsala

¼ cup dry white wine

¼ cup clam juice

¼ cup fish stock

5 tablespoons concentrated Italian tomato paste (in tube)

2 cups cherry tomatoes, halved

2 tablespoons unsalted butter

2 tablespoons minced Italian parsley

Salt and pepper

Place the clams in a large bowl of cold water and swirl them to clean the shells. With a hard brush, scrub the shells, including the joints. Place the cleaned clams in a colander and rinse them under cold water. Drain thoroughly. Repeat the procedure with the mussels.

Start to cook the pasta 5 minutes before you start the sauce. In a large pot bring 6 quarts of water to a boil. Add the 2 tablespoons of coarse salt. Gradually add the pasta and cook for 8 minutes, stirring frequently. Drain the pasta and return it to the pot.

While the pasta is cooking, heat the olive oil in a large skillet over medium-high heat until hot but not smoking. Add the garlic and red pepper flakes and sauté until the garlic turns golden, about 2 minutes; do not brown. Deglaze the pan with the Marsala and white wine, cooking until the liquid has almost evaporated. Add the shellfish and season with salt and pepper to taste. Add the clam juice, fish stock, tomato paste, and cherry tomatoes and simmer for 7 minutes. Add the pasta to the skillet and toss a couple of times; add the butter and cook until it is fully incorporated into the pasta, 2–3 minutes. Discard any unopened mussels or clams. Divide the pasta evenly among 4 warmed plates and sprinkle with the minced parsley. Serves 4.

Wine pairings: Santa Margherita Pinot Grigio; Chateau Ste. Michelle Pinot Gris.

see color plate 18

Watching the horses during a *buskashi* game, Kabul, 1969. Nino Pernetti collection.

FOUR

Afghanistan, Africa, and Asia, 1969–1970

A Different Kind of Cooking

FERDIE: Nino, from the Soviet airliner you could see that the terrain was mountainous, all brown, a gray and arid land, dotted with small villages connected by twisting mountain roads. But it was another big challenge. What was that challenge like?

NINO: I had a two-hour wait before boarding. I sat on a bench stroking my forehead, thanking God and thinking about how much worse the odyssey might have been. Then I went to a store and bought a new pair of pants and a long-sleeved shirt, since the one I was wearing was bloodstained and torn.

My first adventure with the ways of the Afghans involved customs agents. They were curious about my large aluminum trunk still full of my New York, New World suits and other finery. They spread the suits all over a table and were most intrigued by my thirty-some ties in all different colors. As a goodwill gesture I offered one of the guards a tie of his choosing. As the news spread, fifteen other guards showed up for the ties. Following a brief skirmish they went away happy.

The hotel, though not quite finished, was very nice. It sat on the Bagh-i-Bala Hill overlooking Kabul. It was not only the best hotel in Kabul but it was the only international one. However, once again I had run head-on into a language problem. The entire hotel functioned in Farsi. I was assigned an assistant, who took me on a tour of Kabul to get acquainted with the layout of the city. In a two-day tour I saw only a handful of women, wearing the chador, the long, pleated garment with a crocheted veil for the eyes.

FERDIE: No women friends and Farsi to learn. This would be one of your biggest challenges.

NINO: During our tour I watched the city with fascination and wondered about the goings-on. Through the open windows a lot of dust settled on the car's interior, and none of the streets were paved. There were carts with huge wooden wheels being pushed and pulled by men at both ends. There were few motorized vehicles. People in flowing robes roamed the streets on donkeys or camels, and others walked. Most of the houses were made of carved wood or of mud. Bicycles were everywhere. I had not seen a single man wearing a tie, so I was wondering what the customs officers would do with mine. But "cosi è la vita" [such is life].

FERDIE: You were met by the Swiss French general manager, Pierre Martinet, and briefed on Afghan customs and habits. Employment interviews to hire new staff, from top to bottom, were going in earnest. All candidates had one thing in common: they knew only Farsi and refused even to try to learn any other language

NINO: This was going to be hard. In the hotel, there were only male employees, tall men with scars, either from dueling or from the national sport, *buskashi*. It is played on horseback with the aim of gaining possession of a headless calf, and to become a national hero by doing so was each man's goal. The willing staff loved the challenge of creating a spic-and-span European-style spa hotel. I was proud of them.

In 1969 a waiter's pay was a meager fourteen dollars a month, and people worked hard for it. In no time, we had the sharpest staff in all of Kabul. Now the tourists and businessmen had a hotel where the staff greeted them in English, and staff members looked smart in their stylish uniforms. On the front line I put youngsters who wanted to learn the Queen's English. We made weary travelers feel at home by creating an oasis in the desert. Now I applied myself to maintaining high standards.

I began to adjust to the rhythm of life in Kabul. Five times a day most of the staff went to a mosque to pray. Everything stopped. Ramadan was a huge religious observance. I learned that the Afghan people lived by a book of proverbs and old sayings, the most important of which was "God created us, and then forgot about us!"

The hotel was formally opened by the king. I soon found out that it belonged to the government, with only a small managing interest held by InterContinental Hotels. Murphy's Law kicked in on opening day as the king,

Buskashi day, Kabul, 1969. Nino
Pernetti collection.

his family, and their entourage of about sixty people arrived in the lobby, all dressed in black with no smiles on
any faces and profoundly silent, which made it feel more
like a funeral procession than a happy occasion. The
general manager and the king and his family stepped
into the elevator to go the top floor to the Pamir Supper Club. The elevator did not cooperate and stopped
halfway. In under two minutes—which seemed like an
eternity—the problem was fixed. The entire entourage
finally sat down with the royal family at the main table
together with the general manager and the president of
InterContinental Hotels, Mario di Genova, who came
for the occasion.

What had been rehearsed perfectly several times now
went wrong. Evidently, this was Murphy's Law No. 2.
The appetizers were beautifully prepared, jumbo shrimp
cocktail in a nice cocktail glass with all the trimmings.
But since the king's wife did not eat shellfish, the chef
had prepared a similar cocktail with morsels of chicken
to be served to everyone at the main table. A waiter
picked up the tray intended for the main table and

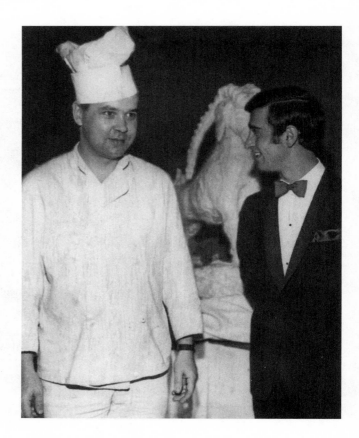

Nino with Chef Burchard in Kabul, 1969. Nino Pernetti collection.

served it to another table. I ran into the dining room to rescue the royal table's chicken cocktails. Alas, they were already in someone else's stomach. I had to go to the main table and inform the general manager of the mishap. Mr. Di Genova raised his eyebrows and fired off in Italian, "Ma che cosa vuol dire questo?" [What kind of bullshit is this?] I ran back to the kitchen and begged executive chef Franz Burchard to prepare more chicken cocktails as fast as he could. The chef laughed—nowhere else in my career was the rivalry between the kitchen and the dining room more evident—and took his sweet time preparing new cocktails. I was picturing myself heading back to Italy and saying "Arrivederci, Kabul."

Mr. Di Genova was known to be very rigorous and precise, not one to tolerate mistakes. The following day, much to my relief, it was the chef who was heading back to Germany. Mr. Di Genova, now lives in Miami and occasionally comes to see me at Caffè Abbracci for a good plate of pasta. This story always comes up, thirty-five years later.

The restaurant was well patronized by the locals and foreigners alike. After all, this was the first Western hotel in Kabul, so the many foreign company executives and embassy and consulate staff members enjoyed our new establishment. We featured local and international dishes with a heavy accent on Italian specialties. The foreign community and businessmen were enchanted that wine and liquor were served with meals, a taboo in other restaurants or at the Khyber Hotel, and they learned about balanced diets and injudicious portions.

In November 1969 I was transferred to the Lusaka InterContinental Hotel in Zambia. I was sorry to see the hard times come to Afghanistan and the hotel. I left many friends behind in Kabul and still wonder how many of them have survived.

FERDIE: How did you react to Africa?

NINO: This time I didn't pack my fine European clothes. I bought those white hunter or British officer's tunics and even had a swagger stick. I was ready for colonialism!

I was glad that everyone spoke English, but the natives spoke Bantu. One day my assistant, Napoleon, asked me, "Bwana, want to hunt crocodiles?" I said yes with great anticipation. He and a waiter came to get me at midnight and I was taken to the Zambezi River. That night was unusually cold, with a full moon. This was typical of the climate in Zambia: very hot during the day and chilly at night. The three of us drove in the waiter's pickup truck. It looked like it would break down any minute. Silently, we drove for a couple of hours on roads that wound through trees and occasional villages of straw houses. At an intersection the driver stopped to pick up two more natives. I did not know who they were nor did they say anything. We all sat in the cab; I was in the middle and could hardly breathe, we were packed so tightly. There was no conversation, only an occasional mumbling in their native dialect. Another hour and we reached our destination. The river looked so calm it could have been a lake. It was breathtaking, incredibly beautiful.

We got off the truck close to the river. On the bank was a kind of canoe made out of a tree trunk approximately six feet long by two feet wide. I asked Napoleon where our boat was. He pointed to the canoe. Now you can imagine five people in that little floating tree! I said, "No thanks, I will stay ashore." It was now 2:30 a.m. with the moonlight shining upon the huge river. I was warned not to wander into the jungle because it was full of wild animals, not to stay under a tree because a big snake might fall down on me, and not to stay too close to the riverbank because crocodiles might grab one of my legs and pull me into the water. At once my hands and face began to sweat profusely.

The four hunters got into the canoe and with flashing lights drew near a couple of crocodiles. As I was staring at them, behind me a wild fight was going on, animals screaming and running, complete pandemonium. I tried to be brave, but I started to panic for in front of my eyes two of the men were wrestling in the water with a crocodile. The boat was waggling, splashing, while the men on board were shouting I don't know what. I really thought these were my last moments on earth, for it appeared the crocodiles were overcoming the hunters and I would be left stranded somewhere in the jungle three hours from civilization. Fortunately, the two men in the water were able to subdue the crocodile and bring it ashore.

I told Napoleon this was a very dangerous and crazy mission, and with a big smile on his face he said, "Not actually, simply a different definition of danger. Sometimes the crocodile with its strong tail hits the canoe and someone always falls in the water. After that someone else must jump in rapidly and grab the crocodile's mouth to keep the other man from being bitten." Once ashore they had to cut open the crocodile's stomach to kill it and to make it lighter to carry. This process had to be done very fast because the smell of blood attracted wild animals. We all jumped into the pickup truck, Napoleon and the waiter and me in the front and the other two in the back with the crocodile. The silence was blissful.

FERDIE: It was Easter weekend and you were sent to the town of Livingstone to help at the InterContinental Mosi-Oa-Tunya (The Smoke That Thunders) Hotel, located at the foot of Victoria Falls.

NINO: We drove there in the hotel's minibus, since we had to transport some equipment and goods. It was an eight-hour trip through the jungle. Two miles from the hotel I saw the mist of the falls and heard the roar of the water. It was spectacular. There were times on the only road leading to the hotel that you would find hippos taking a nap on the warm pavement. Sometimes you had to wait in the car for hours until their siesta time was over. In fact, road signs warned you to approach curves very slowly as you might find elephants and hippos sunbathing in the middle of the road.

One afternoon there was a snake sleeping in front of the door to my cottage. After trying to no avail to scare it away, I went to the nearby pool attendant for help. He was no more than fifteen years old. To my astonishment, this young man marched bravely toward the long snake. Without hesitation he grabbed the snake by the throat and, with its mouth wide open, he twirled it around his arm. He then walked toward the pool, stuck his arm in

Nino waiting for elephants and hippos to pass, Lusaka, 1970. Nino Pernetti collection.

the water for a minute or so until the snake let loose a few bubbles and there was no more sign of life. With a big smile he said, "Bwana, you can go to your flat now."

Another time the hotel was given three days' notice by Pres. Kenneth Kaunda's personal assistant to cater a lunch for the opening of a textile factory in Ndola, Zambia's second-largest city, in the heart of the copper belt on the border with the Democratic Republic of the Congo.

We needed to both transport and set up food for three hundred people in a place we did not know in terms of space, water, and kitchen. Needless to say, the factory had no air-conditioning. The only information we had was that it was located at Tanzania Avenue near the technical college. In those days a wish from President Kaunda was the same as an order. We were not only working against time but we had to prepare food that would last twelve hours without refrigeration. The chef went berserk, and the food and beverage manager was furious. In Lusaka there were no refrigerated trucks, or even trucks to rent. We had to be creative, so we rented four school buses and found drivers. The party was going to be at 1:00 p.m. on a Sunday 210 miles away. There were no paved roads here.

We left Saturday at midnight and reached our destination about 9:00 a.m. the following day. I was in charge of the convoy of thirty employees on the buses, including cooks, waiters, cleaners, and so on. When we arrived at the factory there was nobody there and the gate had a big padlock on it. In those days there were no cellular phones and no public telephone booths either. We could do nothing but wait. We had breakfast—water and some of the sandwiches meant for the party—while sitting on the street.

It was a nice fall day, and we could see families dressed up to go to church, the ladies in big white hats. The sun started to beat down on us. Though we had parked the buses in the shade I was worried about the food. Most of the staff went to look for "cool" spots under the trees and fell asleep. At 11:00 a.m. a guard showed up in military uniform and opened the gate. I was shown where President Kaunda was going to speak.

I asked the guards where the people were going to sit to eat. I received a chilly stare and understood that it was my business to decide where. As the buffet was being set up, one of the guards, with ten others behind him, picked up plates and started to take food. My reaction was instant. I took the plate away from him and said, "You cannot do this. This food is for invited guests only." The guard looked at me and with fire in his eyes removed his revolver from his holster and put it to my head: "What did you say?"

My heart was beating in my throat but, very calmly and with a big smile, I said, "Take whatever you want; it is fine with me." He smiled and patted my shoulder.

The event went smoothly. Upon my return I informed the general manager of the incident with the guard. He reported it to the president's assistant, and the guard was jailed for one month.

Sundays there was nothing to do but go to the Lusaka crafts market. You could find anything there: crocodile bags and belts, ceramics, wooden furniture, batiks, hand-dyed cloth, handcrafted curios, gemstones, jewelry. It was colorful and lively, well worth a visit. Hundreds of residents carved all day long with the most rudimentary tools and turned out creative and excellently crafted items for sale at reasonable prices. I would watch tourists and locals bargain endlessly and animatedly to the point that I thought a fight was imminent.

The excitement, the adrenaline, was always there when I took a safari tour of the Munda Wanga wildlife sanctuary. There I would see lions, tigers, elephants, primates, and some of the most unusual chameleons in Africa. When you see all of the animals in their natural habitat they look so peaceful and harmless.

If you stayed by the hotel's pool there was always the danger that snakes would slither by and get into your belongings. I hated snakes, so I seldom went to the pool. I saw my first polo game there. It was popular among expatriates. Being a soccer fan I found this sport quite boring, lacking enthusiasm among the spectators and lacking passion at all.

RISOTTO

The Making of Risotto

Risotto is the classic rice dish of northern Italy. Pasta rules as the national dish throughout Italy, but risotto reigns in the North. We have listed here some of the classic preparations and some of the recent creations.

We have included the Risotto with Fresh Truffles recipe. This is by far the best dish to enhance the taste and flavor of the white truffles, the diamonds of gastronomy. The combination of the risotto and the truffles makes an extraordinary culinary delight. The truffle must always be fresh and they come from the little town of Alba in Piedmont. The season is very short, late fall, so that is when you should prepare your risotto. You can use a truffle's slicer for shaving the truffles. You want the truffle cut paper-thin. Exercise only a little pressure when you cut it, because too much force will make the shavings too thick. Risotto is a very nutritional and economical dish, and it can be a meal in itself. The basic preparation is always the same; what changes are the flavors or ingredients.

There are certain rules that must be kept. Never wash the rice, because it will loose its starch. The onions must always be golden but not brown. One must keep stirring to prevent sticking. Always add the broth a little at a time, waiting for the previous pouring to be absorbed. Always add the final pour of the broth before making the consistency softer and softer. Always keep the broth simmering slowly, while you are adding the rice. Keep low boiling, but not too low, otherwise the broth takes longer to be absorbed. The time we give you is basic; you can shorten or you can extend it. Taste a bit of the rice. If you run out of broth, you can add simmering water. Risotto once finished must be eaten immediately.

Serve risotto on warm plates. Keep the plates under running hot water and dry them before use. The quantities are basic, however, you may want to add more butter, oil, or Parmesan to suit your taste, or wait if the mixture is too liquid. If the mixture is getting too dry add more broth or simmering water if you run out of broth. At Caffè Abbracci we use Prosecco wine, which is a dry slightly sparkling wine. In cooking, everything relies on intuition and anticipation. We cook it for 20 minutes, but if you like it mellow, you can cook it up to 30 minutes. Let your good cooking sense guide you. You may have to adjust the heat, from time to time. The risotto has to keep boiling. The risotto must always be creamy and tender on the outside, with each grain still distinct and firm to the bite. The good timing is your sense, because it also depends on your pot and your stove.

You can do it with many other ingredients. Remember, the basic technique never changes. As a final touch, always have freshly grated Parmesan cheese on the table for extra passing.

This is fun and great for little gatherings. "E come si dice a casa mia, con il Risotto sempre è festa. Buon Appetito.""And as we say at home, with the risotto there is always a feast."

Risotto with Grapes

Risotto con Uva

5 cups chicken stock

4 tablespoons unsalted butter, divided

1 tablespoon extra-virgin olive oil

2 tablespoons finely minced onion

1½ cups Italian Arborio rice

1 cup Prosecco

½ cup seedless red grapes, halved

½ cup freshly grated Parmesan cheese, plus more for garnish

2 tablespoons minced Italian parsley

Salt and pepper

Bring the stock to a steady simmer in a saucepan. Heat 2 tablespoons butter and 1 tablespoon olive oil in a 10-inch skillet over moderate heat until hot but not smoking. Add the onion and sauté for 1–2 minutes, until translucent. Using a wooden spoon, stir in the rice for 1 minute, making sure it is well coated with the oil. Add the Prosecco and stir until it is almost completely absorbed, about 1 minute. Add the grapes and begin to add the simmering stock ½ cup at a time, stirring constantly. Wait until each addition is almost completely absorbed before adding the next ½ cup. Reserve ¼ cup of the stock to add at the end. Stir frequently to prevent sticking. After approximately 20 minutes, add ½ cup of the stock.

Remove the pan from the heat, season the risotto with salt and pepper to taste, and immediately add the rest of the butter and stir vigorously until the mixture is well combined. Then add the Parmesan cheese and stir one more time. Sprinkle with Parmesan cheese and parsley. Serves 4.

Wine pairings: Trebbiano d'Abruzzo; Franciscan Chardonnay.

Risotto with Saffron

Risotto alla Milanese

5 cups chicken stock

5 tablespoons unsalted butter, divided

1 teaspoon finely minced onion

1½ cups Italian Arborio rice

½ cup Prosecco

1 tablespoon minced beef marrow

½ teaspoon saffron threads dissolved in ½ cup hot chicken stock

½ cup freshly grated Parmesan cheese

Salt and pepper

Bring the stock to a steady simmer in a saucepan and set aside.

Heat 3 tablespoons of the butter in a 10-inch skillet over moderate heat until hot but not smoking. Add the onion and sauté for 1–2 minutes, until translucent. Using a wooden spoon, stir in the rice for 1 minute, making sure it is well coated with the butter. Add the Prosecco and stir until it is almost completely absorbed, about 1 minute. Add the marrow and saffron and begin to add the simmering stock ½ cup at a time, stirring constantly. Wait until each addition is almost completely absorbed before adding the next ½ cup. Reserve ½ cup of the stock to add at the end. Stir frequently to prevent sticking. After approximately 20 minutes, add the reserved stock.

Remove the pan from the heat, season the risotto with salt and pepper to taste, and immediately add 2 tablespoons butter and stir vigorously until the mixture is well combined. Then add the ½ cup of Parmesan cheese and stir one more time. Sprinkle with the Parmesan cheese. Serves 4.

Wine pairings: Friuli-Venezia Giulia Sauvignon del Collio; Markham Sauvignon Blanc.

Risotto with Seafood

Risotto ai Frutti di Mare

12 medium mussels

12 littleneck clams

5 tablespoons extra-virgin olive oil, divided

1 large garlic clove, minced

4 ounces fresh tuna, cut in ¾-inch chunks

4 ounces swordfish, cut in chunks

8 medium shrimp, shelled and deveined

4 ounces calamari rings

2 bay leaves

½ cup dry white wine

½ cup clam juice

½ cup marinara sauce (see recipe, page 59)

½ cup minced onion

1½ cups Italian Arborio rice

5 cups fish stock

2 tablespoons unsalted butter, softened

1 small tomato, peeled, seeded, and diced

2 tablespoons finely minced Italian parsley

Salt and pepper

Scrub the mussels and clams well, rinsing them several times under cold running water, then set them aside.

Bring the stock to a steady simmer in a saucepan. Heat 3 tablespoons of the oil in a large skillet until hot but not smoking. Add the garlic, stir a few times, then add the tuna, swordfish, shrimp, calamari, and bay leaves. Add the wine and stir until it is almost absorbed, about 1 minute. Add the clam juice and marinara sauce and cook 6–8 minutes, stirring constantly. Season with salt and pepper to taste. Remove the seafood and set aside. Discard any mussels and clams that have not opened. Keep the stock simmering on moderate heat.

Heat 2 tablespoons of butter and the oil in a 10-inch skillet over moderate heat until hot but not smoking. Add the onion and sauté for 1–2 minutes, until translucent. Using a wooden spoon, stir in the rice for 1 minute, making sure it is well coated with the butter and oil. Begin to add the simmering stock ½ cup at a time, stirring constantly. Wait until each addition is almost completely absorbed before adding the next ½ cup. Reserve ½ cup of the stock to add at the end. Stir constantly to prevent sticking. After approximately 20 minutes, add the reserved stock and return the seafood to the pan.

Remove the pan from the heat and add the diced tomato, then stir vigorously until the mixture is well combined. Sprinkle with parsley before serving. Serves 4.

Wine pairings: Piedmont Gavi di Gavi Black Label; Mer Soleil Chardonnay.

Risotto with Strawberries

Risotto alle Fragole

5 cups chicken stock

4 tablespoons unsalted butter, divided

2 tablespoons minced onion

½ cup ripe strawberries, washed, hulls and stems removed, diced

¼ cup red Italian vermouth

½ cup Prosecco

2 cups Italian Arborio rice

½ tablespoons grated Parmesan cheese

2 tablespoons minced Italian parsley

Salt and pepper

Bring the stock to a steady simmer in a saucepan and set aside.

Heat 2 tablespoons of the butter in a 10-inch skillet over moderate heat until hot but not smoking. Add the onion and sauté for 1–2 minutes, until translucent. Add the strawberries and continue cooking until they begin to lose their color. Add the vermouth and the Prosecco and cook until the liquid in the pan is reduced to about 1 tablespoon, about 2 minutes. Using a wooden spoon, stir in the rice for 1 minute, making sure it is well coated with the butter. Begin to add the simmering stock ½ cup at a time, stirring constantly. Wait until each addition is almost completely absorbed before adding the next ½ cup. Reserve ½ cup of the stock to add at the end. Stir constantly to prevent sticking. After approximately 20 minutes, add the reserved stock.

Remove the pan from the heat, season the risotto with salt and pepper to taste, and immediately add the rest of the butter and the Parmesan cheese and stir vigorously until the mixture is well combined. Sprinkle each plate with minced parsley. Serves 4.

Wine pairings: Trebbiano d'Abruzzo; Chardonnay Villatorri Franciscan.

Risotto with Vegetables

Risotto Primavera

2 cups eggplant

2 tablespoons Zucchini

2 tablespoons Red bell pepper

2 tablespoons cap mushrooms

8 ounces imported canned baby green peas, drained

2 tablespoons carrots

5 cups chicken stock

2 tablespoons extra-virgin olive oil, divided

6 tablespoons unsalted butter, divided

¼ cup minced onion

1½ cups Italian Arborio rice

½ cup Prosecco

½ cup concentrated Italian tomato paste (in tube)

½ cup freshly grated Parmesan cheese

1 tablespoon minced fresh Italian parsley

Salt and pepper

Peel and cube the eggplant and place it in a colander. Sprinkle with 1 tablespoon salt and allow to sit for 35 minutes to release excess water. Pat dry with paper towels.

Wash the zucchini, trim the ends, and dice.

Roast a firm and glossy red bell pepper over a gas flame or under a broiler as close to the heat as possible, turning often, until charred all over. Transfer to a paper bag, close loosely, and let it steam for 10 minutes. Working over a strainer set over a bowl, scrape off the charred skin; do not worry if a little stays on the flesh and do not rinse the pepper under water because that will wash away the flavor. Remove the stem, core and seeds. Cut the pepper into thin strips, then cut crosswise into ½-inch pieces.

Pat the mushrooms dry with a paper towel. Remove the stems and discard. Slice the mushrooms. Peel and julienne a small carrot.

Bring the chicken stock to a steady simmer in a saucepan. Heat 1 tablespoon of the oil and 1 tablespoon of the butter in a 10-inch skillet over moderate heat. When the butter begins to foam, add the eggplant. After 5 minutes, add the zucchini, bell pepper, mushrooms, and carrots and cook for 5 minutes. Remove the pan from the heat.

Heat the remaining oil and 2 tablespoons of the butter in another 10-inch skillet over medium heat. Add the onion and sauté for 1–2 minutes, until translucent. Using a wooden spoon, stir in the rice for 1 minute, making sure it is well coated with the butter. Add the Prosecco and stir until it is almost completely absorbed, about 1 minute. Begin to add the simmering stock ½ cup at a time, stirring constantly. Wait until each addition is almost completely absorbed before adding the next ½ cup. Reserve ½ cup of the stock to add at the end. Stir constantly to prevent sticking. After approximately 20 minutes, add the tomato paste, the reserved stock, and the vegetables. Season the risotto with salt and pepper to taste and stir for 1 minute. Add the Parmesan cheese and stir vigorously for 1 minute. Sprinkle each plate with parsley. Serves 4.

Wine pairings: Planeta or Kunde Chardonnay.

Risotto with White Truffle

Risotto al Tartufo Bianco

5½ cups chicken stock

2 tablespoons unsalted butter, divided

1 tablespoon extra-virgin olive oil

3 tablespoons minced onion

1½ cups Italian Arborio rice

1½ cups Prosecco

¼ cup light cream

⅓ cup freshly grated Parmesan cheese

1 fresh white truffle, ½ golf-ball size

Salt and pepper

Bring the stock to a steady simmer in a saucepan and set aside.

Heat the butter and olive oil in a 10–inch skillet over moderate heat until hot but not smoking. Add the onion and sauté for 1–2 minutes, until translucent. Using a wooden spoon, stir in the rice for 1 minute, making sure it is well coated with the butter. Add the Prosecco and stir until it is almost completely absorbed, about 1 minute. Begin to add the simmering stock ½ cup at a time, stirring constantly. Wait until each addition is almost completely absorbed before adding the next ½ cup. Reserve ½ cup of the stock to add at the end. Stir constantly to prevent sticking. After approximately 20 minutes, add the reserved stock and the cream.

Remove the pan from the heat, season the risotto with salt and pepper to taste, and immediately add the Parmesan cheese and stir vigorously until the mixture is well combined. Garnish each plate with truffle shavings. Serves 4.

Wine pairings: Veuve Clicquot Yellow Label.

FIVE

Seoul, South Korea, 1970–1971
Diverse Traditions

FERDIE: After six months in Zambia, Ernesto Barba informed you that you were on the move again, this time to Seoul, South Korea. What was your experience like?

NINO: One thing about the move bothered me. South Korea had beaten and eliminated Italy in the last World Cup in England in 1966. I never saw such energy and speed in a soccer team. All you could see was twenty-two legs of whirling speed, like a bunch of ants. And the part that left me very bitter was that the Koreans apparently had the referee in their corner. The newspapers reported that the Korean team played with more than eleven players; it seemed more like fifteen. I never knew the truth.

Nino with South Korean women in traditional dress, Seoul, 1971. Nino Pernetti collection.

I faced my new challenge with an excited heart. I arrived at Kimpo International Airport on a beautiful day in April. The hotel management sent a representative to meet me at the gate with a big banner which read, "Welcome to Seoul, Signor Pernetti!" The welcoming committee cheered, embraced me, kissed my hand in their ceremonial way, and a few days after I arrived they gave me the grand tour of Seoul.

It was a very spread-out city, like those in America, but no skyscrapers or four-lane highways. It was spring and you could see cherry blossoms, the national flower, everywhere.

I started to work in the Americana Chosun Hotel, the first American hotel in Seoul. My job was to train the staff, devise and set up the restaurant's concepts, and supervise the menus and the food preparation.

FERDIE: You found the Koreans to be hard workers, indefatigable. If they didn't speak English, they made a special effort to learn. But there was rigidity to life.

NINO: The dining hours were different, and back then there was a rigidly enforced curfew, because we are talking the late '60s, at the height of the Cold War. Everyone had to be home by 10:00 p.m., Koreans and foreigners alike. Dinner started at 4:30 p.m., and by 8:00 p.m. the restaurants had started to clear out. It made easy hours for my staff.

We opened the first American-style disco with Philippine bands and psychedelic lights. The all-female staff wore silver wigs, silver skirts and tops, and knee-high boots. The disco was open from 9:00 p.m. until 7:00 a.m. It was good for whoever wanted to stay out, as they could stay there until the curfew was over at 6:00 a.m. It was very popular!

In Zambia I was accustomed to driving on the left side of the road. In Seoul I had to make a quick change and learn to drive on the right side of the road. The city was inundated with cars and buses. There were no subways at that time. There was a constant traffic jam that made Rome look quiet in comparison, like a single-lane highway. The lack of street names and signs, no parking, and the unpredictability of the drivers made driving around Seoul very acrobatic. Bus drivers routinely ran red lights; vehicles rarely stopped at pedestrian cross-

Nino in the lobby of the Chosun Hotel, Seoul, 1970. Nino Pernetti collection.

ings that were not protected by traffic lights. I would stand on the sidewalk in front of the hotel at about 9:00 p.m. looking at the many car pools, minivans, and taxies, everyone shouting, doors banging, people whistling, and hundreds of people hurrying, trying to get into their transportation to make it to their destination in time.

The hotel was sparkling clean, the kitchens were spotless. I made many friends in Seoul. One night Kim Park Chong, a friend and the head of the feared secret police in Seoul, invited me to his home. His driver picked me up at the hotel at 5:00 p.m. to have dinner at 6:30. There were only men at the table, as was the Korean custom. We all sat on the floor with our legs crossed. We drank sake, which after two hours made me tipsy. In the Korean tradition, every member of the table toasted the guest of honor as a sign a friendship. This went on throughout the evening. They were eight men, so you can imagine how much I had to drink. This helped me swallow the raw fish they were serving that evening. I swallowed it without chewing; I simply couldn't keep such smelly fish in my mouth for a long period. When they noticed that I had cleaned my plate they would give me more. So I decided to pretend to chew for a long time to prevent them from giving me more.

Suddenly I realized it was 10:15 p.m., past the curfew. I signaled Kim Park about the time and in terror

Nino with employees and their families during a staff picnic, Seoul, 1971. Nino Pernetti collection.

I said, "The curfew." He gestured to me with a calming smile not to worry; after all, he was a policeman, and an important one, too. The dinner ended at 11:00 p.m. I was taken to the hotel by the driver and Kim Park himself.

The city was deserted. It was a strange feeling because our car was the only one on the road. At one point we were stopped by aggressive military police standing at a blockade with machine guns and flashlights pointed at us. They approached the car and asked why we were on the street. Kim Park immediately showed his badge, and they let us through. At the second blockade the same thing occurred, but this time Kim Park ordered an escort with a marked car.

The Chosun Hotel was the first American hotel in South Korea. The restaurants were always packed, as we brought in a variety of Australian and Philippine entertainers. But we still had some cultural issues to resolve. A peculiar problem concerned a traditional Korean food, kimchee, cabbage marinated in garlic, which Koreans eat with everything. The result was that everyone stank from the garlic, and we were receiving many complaints from non-Korean customers. We stopped serving kimchee to the staff. The employees grumbled but the hotel smelled better.

In the rooftop supper club we regularly featured all-girl reviews. It was the Las Vegas of Seoul. The girls, all from Australia, were tall and great looking. No gambling. At the American military base I befriended and consequently hired Michael Pope to be the master of ceremonies for each show and any other event held at the hotel. He did this in exchange for meals. Michael was military and a newscaster on American television in Seoul. He had a charismatic baritone voice, perfect for the emcee of our shows.

Finally the foreign community had food it was familiar with, and it was music to their stomachs. I started up a soccer team here, too, and this was where I had my best time. I was their coach-player, and the team was highly disciplined, well conditioned, and intelligent. We won tournaments, and it resulted in a tight bonding of all the employees.

Seoul was an intriguing city transforming itself from the old Yi dynasty (a capital of the Hermit Kingdom) to a major mover and shaker on the international scene, especially in the fields of commerce and sports.

Twice a year the hotel held a staff picnic, an old Korean tradition. This was a farewell to the season and a hello to the new season. We would drive through amazingly colorful forests, rivers, and mountains. They were great fun-filled celebrations. Every employee would bring his or her family. The wives would dress up in their colorful *hanbok* dress. Each staff member would introduce me to his or her family. No one spoke much English, but they would bow as a demonstration of gratitude and respect. After lunch everyone would give a special performance of their individual talent.

Every weekend during the summer we had fashion shows at the pool with Philippine entertainment, live music, a brunch buffet, and Australian divers performing in the swimming pool. It was the beginning of South Korea's economic boom. The bars and restaurants were heavily patronized. Koreans longed to see a bit of Western culture. Korea was a male-oriented society. In fact, marriage back then was often arranged. The families of

Kim Park Chong *(far right)*, head of the secret police, Seoul, 1970. Nino Pernetti collection.

the future bride and groom took leading roles in arranging a match, sometimes when the prospective bride and groom were only teenagers. My assistant, Kim Park, was married in this fashion, and he told me that he was only ten when he was shown a photograph of the woman his parents had decided he would marry. I tried to discuss this practice with him, but it was too sensitive a subject to talk about. He only said that he was proud of this Korean custom. You would never see a woman smoke, drink, or raise her voice because this was regarded as bad manners.

Nino singing at a staff picnic, Seoul, 1971. Nino Pernetti collection.

Nino's farewell party, Seoul, 1971. Nino Pernetti collection.

Hotel staff and friends at Nino's departure from Kimpo International Airport, Seoul, 1971. Nino Pernetti collection.

My honeymoon in Seoul lasted for one year, and it went by in a flash. I was happy and at the same time sad to have to move on. In the Korean tradition, it is customary, when a leader or important family member departs on a long journey, for the most devoted persons to share the last night and sleep in the same room as a sign of respect and fraternity. It was to become a giant party in my hotel room, with twenty-five of my close assistants, supervisors, and other employees. They all slept on the floor and in the bathroom. The following day, in a big caravan, everybody drove together to Kimpo International Airport, and each person offered me a small gift of remembrance. It was a very emotional moment for me. As I crossed through passport control they all started to sing. I left behind a lot of friends with big hearts.

POULTRY

Chicken with Balsamic Vinegar and Red Wine

Pollo al Balsamico e Vino Rosso

32 small chicken thighs, skinned

3 teaspoons extra-virgin olive oil

½ cup minced shallots

1½ tablespoons minced fresh thyme

1 teaspoon fresh rosemary

½ cup Cabernet

1 cup Modena balsamic vinegar

½ cup chicken stock

¼ cup honey

1 bay leaf

4 medium tomato roses

8 arugula leaves, for garnish

1 tablespoon minced Italian parsley

Salt and pepper

Preheat the oven to 350°F.

Season the chicken with salt and pepper. Heat the olive oil in an ovenproof braising pan over medium-high heat until hot but not smoking. Brown the chicken on all sides until it is a deep, golden color, about 5 minutes per side. Transfer it to a plate.

Add the shallots, thyme, and rosemary to the pot and sauté until the shallots are soft and golden. Pour the Cabernet into the pan and scrape up any bits left from the chicken. Cook 1–2 minutes, until nearly all the liquid has evaporated.

Add the balsamic vinegar, chicken stock, honey, bay leaf, and chicken to the pot and bring to a simmer. Cover and transfer the pan to the oven. Bake 30 minutes, turning once.

Remove the pan from the oven and transfer the chicken to a platter; cover with foil and keep warm. Remove the bay leaf and skim off any fat on the surface of the sauce. Transfer the sauce to a skillet and cook over medium-high heat until it is reduced by half and has reached the consistency of light syrup. Divide the chicken evenly among 4 warmed plates and spoon the sauce over it. Garnish with the tomato rose and arugula and sprinkle with parsley. Serves 4.

Wine pairings: Frescobaldi Chianti Classico Nippozano Riserva; Francis Coppola Claret.

see color plate 19

Chicken with Asiago and Prosciutto

Pollo con Asiago e Prosciutto

4 boneless, skinless chicken breast halves

All-purpose flour, for dredging

6 tablespoons unsalted butter, divided

¼ cup chicken stock

½ cup finely grated Asiago

8 fresh sage leaves

8 Italian prosciutto slices

⅔ cup dry white wine

Salt and pepper

Preheat the oven to 375°F.

Season the chicken breasts with salt and pepper to taste. Dredge in flour, shaking off the excess.

Melt 4 tablespoons of the butter in a large skillet over medium heat. Sauté the chicken breasts until brown, turning once, about 5 minutes. Transfer the chicken to a rimmed baking sheet and pour the stock over the chicken. Sprinkle 2 tablespoons of Asiago over each chicken breast and top each with 2 sage leaves and 2 prosciutto slices. Bake until the chicken is cooked through, about 20 minutes.

While the chicken is baking, in the same skillet melt 2 tablespoons butter and add the wine. Bring the mixture to a boil, scraping up any browned bits, until the sauce is reduced to ⅓ cup, about 4 minutes.

Divide the chicken among 4 warmed plates and pour the sauce over it. Serves 4.

Wine pairings: Felsina Chianti Classico; Estancia Estates Pinot Noir.

Chicken with Smoked Mozzarella

Pollo con Mozzarella Affumicata

4 7-ounce boneless, skinless chicken breast halves

¼ cup oil-packed sun-dried tomatoes, drained

6 leaves fresh basil, minced

½ cup chopped pine nuts

1 cup diced smoked Italian mozzarella

Extra-virgin olive oil, for drizzling

Salt and pepper

Using a meat mallet, pound each chicken breast half to a half-inch thickness. Season with salt and pepper to taste and set aside.

Preheat the oven to 375°F. In a food processor combine the sun-dried tomatoes, basil, pine nuts, and mozzarella. Pulse until everything is uniformly mixed. Spread some of the mixture on each chicken breast and roll it up. Tie each roll with butcher's twine. Drizzle each roll with olive oil and wrap it in parchment paper. Place the rolls on a baking sheet and bake for 30 minutes. Remove the baking sheet from the oven and set it aside to cool slightly before unwrapping the bundles. When the chicken bundles are cool enough to handle, remove the butcher's twine and cut each roll into thick slices. Serves 4.

Wine pairings: Cá del Bosco Bianco di Franciacorta; Cosentino Merlot.

Chicken with Prosciutto and Fontina

Pollo con Prosciutto e Fontina

4 7-ounce boneless, skinless chicken breast halves

All-purpose flour, for dredging

4 slices Italian prosciutto

4 tablespoons unsalted butter, divided

2 tablespoons extra-virgin olive oil

⅓ cup dry white wine

½ cup chicken stock

4 thin slices Italian fontina

2 tablespoons tomato sauce (see recipe, page 61)

Salt and pepper

Preheat the oven to 375°F.

Dredge the chicken breasts in flour to coat lightly and tap off excess flour. Lay each chicken breast flat on the work surface and cover with a slice of prosciutto. Gently pound the prosciutto into the chicken so it adheres better.

Heat 2 tablespoons of butter and the olive oil in a large ovenproof skillet until the butter foams. Place the chicken breasts prosciutto side down in the skillet; they should not touch. Season with salt and pepper to taste. Cook for 2 minutes; longer cooking will toughen the prosciutto. Turn the chicken and cook until the other side is golden brown, about 3 minutes. Pour the wine into the skillet and boil until it is reduced by half. Add the chicken stock and the remaining 2 tablespoons butter and season with salt and pepper to taste. Bring to a boil, lower the heat, and let the sauce simmer, tilting the skillet to mix the ingredients.

Place a slice of fontina over each chicken breast to cover completely. Dot the center of each chicken breast with tomato sauce. Place the skillet in the oven and bake until the chicken is cooked through and the sauce is bubbling, about 12 minutes. Serve on warmed plates. Serves 4.

Wine pairings: Cá del Bosco Bianco di Franciacorta; Cosentino Merlot.

A poolside party at the Condesa del Mar, Acapulco, 1972. Nino Pernetti collection.

SIX   *Acapulco, Mexico, 1971–1973*
              Education in Hotel Entertainment

FERDIE: Nino, the home office transferred you to Acapulco, Mexico, as food and beverage director of the soon-to-open Americana Condesa del Mar Hotel. If the geography was stunning, the hotel outshone everything else. It was majestic, an architectural crown jewel. Was it the best?

NINO: As far as I was concerned, it was the top of the line. The people who frequented the hotel were the best of the U.S., Europe, and Mexico.

For the first six months I did not take a day off. I didn't want to be away from the hotel, it was so good, so much fun. I had to be ordered to take a day off. There was dazzling nightlife, diverse cuisine, and local shopping to please just about anybody. Exuberant by day, brilliant by night, the city was one long fiesta.

FERDIE: The nearby Villa Vera Tennis Club, sitting on the hills, its pool overlooking Acapulco Bay, was famous for hosting the jet set. Whom did you meet?

NINO: I befriended Farrah Fawcett on the tennis court and became chummy with Elvis Presley. He was with his girlfriend, Linda Thompson, and they were head over heels in love.

In early autumn 1965, when I was working as a waiter at the Bauer Grünwald Hotel in Venice, I had the rare pleasure of meeting Elvis Presley and his then-girlfriend (and future wife) Priscilla. I served him breakfast twice, and Elvis took time to chat with me, one-on-one, like two guys talking. I was overwhelmed, but he did most of the talking. In Acapulco I spotted him at the wet bar and approached him to see if he remembered me.

Elvis was very good-looking. His jet-black hair combed back off his face was very impressive to me. His best feature was an easy, big smile. Oh, I could see how the world of women was at his feet. I remember that during one of our conversations I told him I had been working in Frankfurt, among many other places, and he laughed easily and said that was where he was stationed and where he met his wife, Priscilla, when she was only fourteen. He told me he was in the midst of a divorce and so he couldn't talk about her at the moment, but he was enjoying Acapulco and said he always had a great time there. He had been there while making his thirteenth movie, *Fun in Acapulco*. He said the movie did well and thirteen was his lucky number. That reminded me of the gift Mr. Risatti had given me for my birthday many years before: the key ring with the number 13 on it. Maybe that was an omen for me, meaning good luck in the near future.

Elvis wore a long gold chain around his neck with a disk on it engraved with a tree. "This is my tree of life," he said, and he seemed to put a lot of faith in it. On each branch was engraved the name of the most important people in his life, and on the reverse side he had inscribed a Bible verse in three languages: English, Hebrew, and Latin.

While we were speaking, his assistant gave him two green bottles of water. "This is my Mountain Valley mineral water. This is the only water I drink when I'm on the road. I always take cases of water with me. I feel safe this way." He called his assistant to bring me one also.

"Would you like to play tennis?" I asked.

"Yes, but not when it's so hot like today. I sweat too much on stage already, and I can't afford to lose more fluids in a game." As we parted he gave me a special invitation to come to Vegas to see him sing at the Hilton. Of course I went. How could I not?

Elvis was one of the great entertainers of our time. He held the audience in the palm of his hand. A few months later I went to see his performance in Las Vegas and was enthralled but did not go backstage to see him, as I thought that he would not remember me. Now I know I should've gone. Even if Elvis had not recalled our meetings, he was too much of a gentleman to have said so, and he would have made me feel like his friend. I consider myself lucky to have known Elvis Presley in his prime. He was a prince of players!

Nino at buffet with Chef Umberto, Acapulco, 1971. Nino Pernetti collection.

FERDIE: Always at the Villa Vera Tennis Club there was someone famous. On one occasion you noticed Tom Jones taking a lemonade break from a tennis match and conversed with you about his little hometown, Pontypridd, in Wales, and how he started his career as a singer while working in a coal mine.

NINO: Life was a dream. Every day there was a different face, a different celebrity. I was included in every party, and every night there was a party. I loved it.

It was three weeks before Easter and all of Acapulco was going to be fully booked. Most wealthy Mexicans spent the holidays in Acapulco, where they owned beach villas or stayed in luxury hotels. So Mexico City was going to be empty. At our sister hotel in Mexico City, the Fiesta Palace, at the Stellaris Supper Club, the resident singer was none other than Julio Iglesias. He performed there four nights a week. Since during Easter week the supper club was going to close, the French hotel impresario Bernard Meder came to me to offer Julio Iglesias for that week. Well, Julio hadn't hit the northern hemisphere yet, but he was big in Mexico, and his records sold like Elvis's. I was ignorant of who he was and turned the offer down; I was afraid he would not fill the ballroom of the hotel. But Monsieur Meder persisted.

I had heard of a singer named Iglesias and I thought (I had just started to learn Spanish) he meant a man who sang in church. [*Iglesias* means churches in Spanish.] When Mr. Meder assured me that Julio would pack the room and when he hummed some of his songs, I immediately recognized "Canto a Galicia," a huge hit in Europe. He won the European Music Festival award with this song.

FERDIE: So once you heard the song you realized what a big mistake you had made. You met the very charismatic Señor Iglesias, and you were delighted to find that he was fluent in Italian.

NINO: As a Spaniard and an Italian the first thing we talked about was soccer, as our countries have a long-standing passion for the sport. I learned that Julio had had a stint with the famous Real Madrid team as a goalkeeper. We finished the pleasantries and got down to business. Needless to say, we closed the deal in the blink of an eye. Julio was to perform Friday, Saturday, and Easter Sunday, two shows a night in the hotel's ballroom, the first show with dinner, the second show with drinks. For both shows we had a cover charge. We then

Nino with Julio Iglesias at a charity event, Miami, 1988. Photo by Alberto Puigi.

Ferrante and Teicher, Acapulco, 1971. Nino Pernetti collection.

went for lunch at Los Corrales coffee shop overlooking the pool.

I asked the art director to design a poster announcing the show at our hotel. A couple of days after placing the poster in the lobby, the front desk manager was ringing my office telling me there were a dozen people wanting to purchase tickets. I was pleasantly surprised. It was like going fishing and throwing your bait into the water and catching a fish right away. I drew a temporary ticket on stationery and told my secretary to make copies and to make them into tickets. The show sold out. Julio and his family arrived on a Monday afternoon from Mexico City. A few rehearsals and we were ready to go.

A full-capacity crowd was ready for the show. I stepped on stage to announce the great Julio Iglesias, and to much applause the tanned and handsome Julio came on stage. The women went wild, the audience was hysterical. He did a couple of songs whispering melodically through the microphone.

All the while the waiters were serving, as it was a dinner show. Suddenly, Julio stopped singing. He stayed motionless onstage. I asked him what was wrong and he replied, "I don't sing while the waiters are serving. They make too much noise and the audience cannot hear my singing." I ordered the waiters to stop serving until the star had finished singing. Julio grinned. I had made a friend.

Halfway through the first show, the microphone went out. I saw Julio standing still in the spotlight swinging his microphone like a pendulum around and around in absolute silence. The microphone cable had snapped loose without anyone realizing it when a technician inadvertently stepped on it. I saved the day by reconnecting the cable.

Television star Raúl Velasco, host of *Siempre en Domingo*, despite his popularity, was a very simple man. He was a regular at the hotel. On one weekend in 1972, while he was enjoying a piña colada at the pool with his family, I asked him, "Raúl, if I got a top Italian designer and professional models for a fashion show gala around the hotel pool, would you be interested in being our master of ceremonies?" Having Raúl Velasco as the emcee would guarantee success. With a smile and astonishing generosity he said, "Nino, just give me the penthouse for that weekend for me and my family, pay the travel expenses, and providing you have a fashion house with a good name, I will be your emcee." His

Fashion designer Ken Scott *(center)* with models wearing his designs, Acapulco, 1972. Nino Pernetti collection.

darling wife looked at me and said, "Nino, you're a lucky man." We shook hands and I went to my office. After five weeks of telephone calls, telexes, and letters to Italy I was able to secure the House of Ken Scott from Milan, a designer in demand by fashion fanatics.

Ken Scott was famous for his daring and colorful design-prints on fine-quality dresses. I traveled to Italy and went to his office on the third floor above his show-room at the fashionable Via Montenapoleone No. 5 in Milan. I told him of my plan to hold a mega fashion show in Acapulco with press, TV, invited personalities, and artists. All expenses would be paid but there would be no other compensation. And it would introduce his designs to this part of the world. He said, "You picked the right month but the wrong year."

I did not give up. The very next day, while he and I were having a nice plate of linguine with clams at the popular restaurant the Paper Moon in Milan, I used my best skills to persuade him. Ken agreed to the terms and, to my surprise, told me that he was familiar with Mexico because he owned a house in Cuernavaca. He would come with six models and five staff members. Now I had to find an underwriter.

On my return I met with the Alitalia representative for the United States in Los Angeles, Signor Vittorio Vollari. In exchange for Alitalia being the major spon-sor, he agreed to comp the tickets from Milan to Los Angeles.

I was so excited I couldn't sleep that night. For a mo-ment I thought the event was becoming too big for me. I had a lot of work to do, coordinating and following up on all the details. Once back in Acapulco I told the gen-eral manager, Mr. Claude Gautier, what I had achieved. He was flabbergasted. While stroking his chin and with a fatherly look, he said to me, "Nino, if you pull this off, as a reward I will send you to the hotel summer courses at Cornell University in Ithaca, New York, for four months." For me, the motivation doubled instantly.

My next step was to find a cosponsor to pick up the tab for the cost of the trip from Los Angeles to Aca-pulco. I visited the office of the sales director for Aero-naves de México in Acapulco. Manuel Machorro and

I were good friends, as we played tennis together. He accepted my proposal to be the cosponsor of the fashion show.

I hired the best company in Mexico City to build the stage, catwalk, and lighting and to design the sound. The hotel's public relations department sent invitations to the mayor of Acapulco, the mayor of Mexico City, plus local movie and television stars. This night would have Raúl Velasco on stage with Armando Manzanero singing, Julio Iglesias applauding along with Marco Antonio Muñiz, and Pedro Vargas. The night before, colorful floodlights illuminated the hotel and there were spectacular fireworks. The following day headlines named it the event of the year under the skies of Acapulco where eight hundred people would live a fairy tale. To this day, when Raúl Velasco comes to Caffè Abbracci we recall that night of a "thousand and one nights." I did get to attend Cornell University and received a diploma that hangs on my office wall today at Caffè Abbracci.

Once I was invited to a fiesta in a little village about three hours from the hotel. The dinning room captain, Andrés, wanted to show me what life was like in the villages and also to introduce me to his family. They had a huge table loaded with food, mariachis playing, and people dancing the traditional Mexican dances.

Around 8:00 p.m. everyone watched a film. We all moved to the side where the movie was to be shown. "We reserved this seat for you," said Andrés. I was

Nino with Armando Manzanero, Acapulco, 1972. Nino Pernetti collection.

Nino and the Condesa del Mar soccer team, Acapulco, 1972. Nino Pernetti collection.

flattered to be sitting in the first row. I was already exhausted by the long day but I sat down in front of a white sheet covering a wall, which would serve as the screen. I noticed that the wall not covered by the sheet was full of holes and scratches: "Why is the wall full of holes?"

"Oh, many people are armed, and when they see a film with a villain, they shoot at him on the screen," Andrés said. I made a quick calculation. Being close to the screen, the trajectory of the bullets would be inches above my head. I made up an excuse to move to the back row. I enjoyed the movie in tranquility. No shots, though!

As during my previous assignments, soccer came into my life again. I started up a hotel soccer team, again as coach-player. After a few months in Acapulco a rumor began to circulate that, if you weren't a good soccer player, you wouldn't get a job at the Condesa del Mar. To say this hotel's team was overly aggressive is an understatement.

As always in the management field, work ends in one place and new work begins in another. After a year and a half of excitement and fun I had to move on. I was offered the opportunity to work at the Merlin Hotel in Kuala Lumpur, Malaysia. Now my Indian Ocean adventures would begin.

Plate 1. Carpaccio of Beef

Plate 2. Carpaccio of Salmon

Plate 3. Crostini with Pear and Prosciutto

Plate 4. Cured Beef with Goat Cheese

Plate 5. Mussels with Smoked Beef

Plate 6. Polenta with Shiitake Mushrooms and Gorgonzola

Plate 7. Seafood Salad with Red Bell Pepper Purée

Plate 8. Shrimp with Fresh Beans

Plate 9. Fettuccine with Boiled Prosciutto

Plate 10. Fusilli with Eggplants

Plate 11. Fusilli with Italian Sausage

Plate 12. Fusilli with Ricotta

Plate 13. Linguini with Shrimp

Plate 14. Orecchiette with Broccoli Rabe

Plate 15. Penne with Broccoli and Porcini Mushrooms

Plate 16. Penne with Pancetta and Saffron

Plate 17. Penne with Pumpkin and Yogurt

Plate 18. Spaghetti with Shellfish

Plate 19. Chicken with Balsamic Vinegar and Red Wine

Plate 20. Corvina (California Blue Fish) with Basil and Mustard

Plate 21. Mahi mahi with Lemon and Capers

Plate 22. Salmon with Pesto

Plate 23. Shrimp with Tomatoes and Goat Cheese

Plate 24. Swordfish with Anchovy-Balsamic Marinade

Plate 25. Swordfish with Fennel and Basil

Plate 26. Tilapia with White Wine and Truffle Oil

Plate 27. Tuna with Olives and Gherkin Relish

Plate 28. Yellowtail with Artichokes

Plate 29. Sirloin Steak with Gorgonzola Sauce

Plate 30. Beef Tenderloin with Aromatic Herbs

Plate 31. Lamb Chops with Dried Cherries and Berries

Plate 32. Pork Tenderloins with Balsamic-Plum Sauce

Plate 33. Veal Chops with Grapes and Marsala

Plate 34. Veal Scaloppine with Prosciutto and Arugula

Plate 35. Veal Tenderloins with Mushrooms

Plate 36. Pears with Chocolate Sauce

Plate 37. Zabaglione with Wild Berries

Photos by Derek Cole

FISH & SEAFOOD

Corvina (California Blue Fish) with Basil and Mustard

Corvina al Basilico e Mostarda

20 basil leaves, minced

1 garlic clove, minced

½ tablespoon Champagne mustard

2 egg yolks

1 cup extra-virgin olive oil

2 tablespoons fresh lemon juice

4 6-ounce fresh corvina fillets

½ cup water

2 tablespoons dry white wine

¼ cup fish stock

2 tablespoons clam juice

4 large romaine lettuce leaves

1 medium tomato rose

Salt and pepper

In a large bowl blend the basil, garlic, mustard, and egg yolks, using a whisk. Add the oil a little at a time, whisking constantly, until a soft mayonnaise-like cream is obtained. Add salt to taste and lemon juice and blend well. Set aside.

Clean the fish fillets under cold running water. Pat them dry with paper towels and season with salt and pepper to taste. In a saucepan over medium-high heat combine the water, wine, fish stock, and clam juice, and stir a few times; add the fillets. Cook 5–6 minutes. Remove the fillets from the pan and turn off the heat.

Scald the lettuce leaves in the fish-cooking liquid and then spread them out on a warmed serving platter. Place the fillets atop the lettuce leaves and pour the dressing over them. Garnish with the tomato rose. Serve on warmed plates.

Serves 4.

Wine pairings: Friuli-Venezia Giulia Pinot Bianco del Collio; Geyser Peak Chardonnay.

see color plate 20

Corvina (California Blue Fish) with Onion Sauce

Filetti di Corvina con Salsa di Cipolle

4 large yellow onions

4 6-ounce fresh corvina fillets

8 tablespoons extra-virgin olive oil, divided

4 tablespoons diced Italian pancetta

1 teaspoon hot paprika

2 tablespoons minced fresh Italian parsley

Salt and pepper

Preheat the oven to 375°F.

Place the unpeeled onions on a baking sheet and bake for approximately an hour, or until soft.

Clean the fish fillets under cold running water. Pat the fillets dry with paper towels, then season with salt and pepper to taste. Heat 1 tablespoon olive oil in a large, heavy skillet over medium-high heat until hot but not smoking. Add the fillets and cook for 5–6 minutes, turning once, until tender and browned on both sides. Remove the fillets from the skillet and keep them warm.

In a small skillet over moderate heat, heat 1 tablespoon olive oil until hot but not smoking and brown the pancetta, approximately 2 minutes. Remove the skillet from the heat.

Peel the onions and place them in a blender; season with salt and pepper to taste, the paprika, and the remaining olive oil. Purée until a thick paste forms.

Place the fillets on warmed plates. Pour the onion sauce over them, then divide the pancetta evenly among the plates. Sprinkle each plate with parsley. Serves 4.

Wine pairings: Vernaccia di San Gimignano; Taz Chardonnay.

Dover Sole with Citrus Sauce

Sogliola agli Aromi Cittrici

7 tablespoons fresh orange juice, strained

6 tablespoons fresh lemon juice, strained

2 2-inch strips orange zest, julienned

10 black Italian Gaeta olives, pitted and quartered

¼ cup dry white wine

8 3-ounce Dover sole fillets

2 tablespoons fish stock

1 tablespoon clam juice

2 teaspoons minced fresh sage

2 teaspoons minced fresh rosemary

2 tablespoons unsalted butter

3 tablespoons minced fresh Italian parsley

Salt and pepper

In an ovenproof dish large enough to hold the fillets in one layer, stir together the orange juice, lemon juice, orange zest, olives, and wine. Add the fillets, coating them well with the mixture, and let them marinate for 20 minutes in the refrigerator.

Preheat the oven to 350°F.

Remove fillets from marinate. In a clean baking dish, brush with butter and add fillets. Place the fish in the oven and cook for 4–5 minutes. Turn off the heat. Remove the fillets from the dish, place them on a platter, cover with foil, and place the platter in the oven.

Transfer the orange juice mixture to a sauté pan and add the fish stock, clam juice, sage, and rosemary. Cook until the mixture thickens slightly, about 10 minutes, stirring occasionally. Add the butter and cook for 2 minutes, stirring until it is incorporated. Force the mixture through a fine-mesh sieve into a bowl.

Divide the fillets among 4 warmed plates, spoon the orange juice mixture over each fillet, and sprinkle each plate with parsley. Serves 4.

Wine pairings: Lagaria or Taz Chardonnay.

Grouper with Black Olives and Tomatoes

Cernia al Forno con Olive Nere e Pomodori

6 large tomatoes

¼ cup extra-virgin olive oil,
plus 2 tablespoons

1 onion, minced

4 7-ounce fresh grouper
fillets

¼ cup water

2 garlic cloves, crushed

25 black Italian Gaeta olives,
pitted and halved lengthwise

Salt and pepper

Preheat the oven to 300°F.

Bring a large pan of water to a boil; plunge the tomatoes into the boiling water and cook until the skins begin to loosen, about 2 minutes (no longer). Remove the tomatoes from the boiling water with a wire skimmer and place them in an ice water bath for a minute; remove the skin. Using a fork to avoid handling the tomatoes too much, cut the tomatoes in quarters. Squeeze out the seeds and dice.

Heat 2 tablespoons olive oil in a large skillet until hot but not smoking. Add the onions and cook until lightly browned 1-2 minutes. Add the tomatoes, season with salt and pepper to taste, and cook over medium-low heat for 10 minutes.

Pat the fillets dry with paper towels. Place them in an ovenproof ceramic or glass dish and season with salt and pepper to taste. Pour the remaining olive oil, the water, and the garlic over the fish, then distribute the tomato sauce and olives in the pan. Bake for 25 minutes.

Place the fillets on warmed plates and top with the baking sauce. Serves 4.

Wine pairings: Gavi di Gavi Black Label; Ferrari Carano Chardonnay.

Mahi mahi with Lemon and Capers

Mahimahi ai Capperi e Limone

⅓ cup fresh lemon juice

1 tablespoon minced Italian parsley

1 tablespoon chopped fresh chives

1 teaspoon capers, rinsed and drained

3 tablespoons extra-virgin olive oil, divided

4 6-ounce fresh mahimahi fillets

¼ cup all-purpose flour

1 tablespoon fish stock

2 tablespoons dry white wine

12 chives, for garnish

Salt and pepper

In a small bowl, stir together the lemon juice, parsley, minced chives, capers, and 2 tablespoons of the olive oil and season with a pinch of salt. Set aside.

Rinse the fish under cold running water and pat it dry with paper towels; season with salt and pepper to taste. Place the flour on a flat plate and dredge the fish on both sides, shaking off the excess.

Heat the remaining tablespoon of oil in a large skillet over medium-high heat until hot but not smoking. Add the fillets in a single layer and cook 4–5 minutes, turning once, until tender and browned on both sides. Stir in the fish stock and wine and cook for 2 minutes.

Place the fillets in the center of warmed plates, drizzle with the lemon mixture, and garnish with chives. Serves 4.

Wine pairings: Lagaria or Taz Chardonnay.

see color plate 21

Salmon with Pesto

Salmone al Pesto

½ cup pine nuts

Pesto sauce (see recipe, page 60; add 1 cup minced fresh Italian parsley to recipe)

1 tablespoon extra-virgin olive oil

4 6-ounce fresh salmon fillets

Salt and pepper

Preheat the oven to 350°F.

Place the pine nuts on a small rimmed baking sheet and toast until golden brown, about 5 minutes; set aside.

Make the pesto sauce.

Heat the olive oil in a large skillet over medium-high heat until hot but not smoking. Sprinkle the fillets with salt and pepper to taste and cook, turning once 4 minutes per side. Remove the fillets from the skillet and place them on a baking sheet. Bake for 4–5 minutes.

Transfer the fillets to warmed plates and top with the pesto sauce. Sprinkle with toasted pine nuts. Serves 4.

Wine pairings: Caputo or Campania Greco di Tufo; Robert Mondavi Fumé Blanc

see color plate 22

Sea Bass with Olives and White Truffle Oil

Spigola alle Olive Verdi e Olio di Tartufo Bianco

4 6-ounce fresh sea bass fillets

3 tablespoons extra-virgin olive oil, divided

4 lemon slices, seeded

¼ cup dry vermouth

¼ cup pitted brine-cured green olives, halved lengthwise

1 tablespoon fresh lemon juice

½ teaspoon dried oregano

½ tablespoon white truffle oil

Salt and pepper

Preheat the oven to 375°F.

Wash the fillets under cold running water. Pat dry with paper towels and season with salt and pepper to taste. Heat 1 tablespoon olive oil in a large heavy skillet over medium-high heat until hot but not smoking. Sear the fillets one side only until browned well, 3–4 minutes. Transfer, seared side up, to a baking dish and top each fillet with a lemon slice.

Add the vermouth to the same skillet and bring it to a boil, scraping up any brown bits. Boil for 40 seconds, then pour it around the fillets. Scatter the olives around and on top of the fillets and bake, uncovered, for 6–8 minutes. Transfer the fillets to a platter and keep warm. Whisk the lemon juice, oregano, truffle oil, and remaining olive oil into the cooking liquid in the baking dish; season with salt and pepper to taste and stir a few times.

Place the fillets on warmed plates and pour the sauce over. Serves 4.

Wine pairings: LivioFelluga Pinot Grigio; Simi Chardonnay.

Shrimp with Tomatoes and Goat Cheese

Scampi con Pomodori e Caprino

7 tablespoons extra-virgin olive oil, divided

1 large onion, chopped

1 medium fennel bulb, trimmed, thinly sliced

¾ teaspoon red pepper flakes

1¼ pounds ripe tomatoes, chopped

1 teaspoon dried oregano

20 large shrimp, peeled and deveined

½ cup dry white wine

6 ounces goat cheese, crumbled (such as Montrachet)

Juice of 1 lemon

1 tablespoon minced Italian parsley, for garnish

Salt and pepper

Heat 4 tablespoons olive oil in large skillet over medium heat until hot but not smoking. Add the onion, fennel, and red pepper flakes and sauté until the vegetables are tender, 5–7 minutes. Add the tomatoes and oregano and season with salt and pepper to taste. Reduce the heat to low and cook 7 minutes. Transfer to a bowl.

Heat the remaining olive oil in a large skillet over medium-high heat until hot but not smoking. Add the shrimp and cook until just pink, about 3 minutes. Add the wine and cook for 2 minutes. Add the vegetables and heat through. Stir in the goat cheese, then the lemon juice.

Remove the shrimp and vegetables to a serving plate and sprinkle with the parsley. Season with salt and pepper to taste. Serves 4.

Wine pairings: Santa Margherita or Trentino–Alto Adige Pinot Grigio; or Ferrari Carano Fumé Blanc.

see color plate 23

Swordfish with Anchovy-Balsamic Marinade

Pescespada con Acciughe e Balsamico

1 cup salted water

4 medium leeks, cut lengthwise, for garnish

½ cup canola oil

2 large garlic cloves, minced

5 oil-packed anchovy fillets, drained and minced

¼ cup Modena balsamic vinegar

2 teaspoons dried oregano

1 teaspoon herbes de Provence

4 6-ounce fresh swordfish fillets

Fresh basil leaves, for garnish

1 medium tomato rose

Salt and pepper

In a small skillet bring the salted water to a boil and add the leeks; cook for 5 minutes. Remove the leeks and set aside.

Heat the canola oil in another small skillet over medium-high heat until hot but not smoking. Add the garlic and sauté 2 minutes. Add the anchovies and whisk until they dissolve, about 2 minutes. Remove the pan from the heat and cool 1 minute. Whisk in the vinegar, oregano, and herbes de Provence. Season with salt and pepper to taste.

Heat the grill (or a nonstick square grill pan) to medium-hot. Season the fillets with salt and pepper to taste and brush with 2 tablespoons of the anchovy dressing. Grill the fillets until cooked through, about 4 minutes per side. Pass the remaining dressing separately. Serves 4.

Wine pairings: Santa Margherita Pinot Grigio; Robert Mondavi Fumé Blanc.

see color plate 24

Swordfish with Fennel and Basil

Pescespada con Finocchio e Basilico

14 tablespoons unsalted butter, divided

3 small fennel bulbs, trimmed, thinly sliced

4 tablespoons minced fresh mint, divided

4 tablespoons julienned fresh basil leaves, divided

4 6-ounce fresh swordfish fillets

1 cup fish stock

¼ cup dry white wine

½ cup clam juice

¼ cup dry vermouth

Salt and pepper

Preheat the oven to 400°F.

Melt 4 tablespoons butter in a heavy, medium ovenproof skillet over medium heat until the butter foams. Add the fennel, cover, and cook, stirring occasionally, about 6 minutes. Add 1 tablespoon each of mint and basil. Season with salt and pepper to taste. Transfer to plates and keep warm.

Melt 4 tablespoons butter in the same skillet over high heat until the butter foams. Season the fillets with salt and pepper to taste and place in the skillet. Cook 1 minute; turn and cook an additional minute. Place the skillet in the oven and bake the fillets about 4 minutes. Place the fillets atop the fennel and herbs. Cover with foil.

Add the stock, wine, clam juice, vermouth, and 2 tablespoons each of mint and basil to the same skillet. Boil until the liquid is reduced, about 8 minutes. Strain into a bowl. Return the strained liquid to the skillet. Add 6 tablespoons butter and 1 tablespoon each of mint and basil; whisk just until the butter melts.

Place the fillets on warmed plates and pour the stock mixture over the fish. Top the fillets with the fennel. Serves 4.

Wine pairings: Tiefenbruner Pinot Grigio; Chateau St. Jean Fumé Blanc

see color plate 25

Tilapia with White Wine and Truffle Oil

Tilapia al Vino Bianco e Olio di Tartufo

4 6-ounce fresh tilapia fillets

2 tablespoons unsalted butter, plus extra for buttering the pan

½ teaspoon all-purpose flour

1 cup fish stock

1 teaspoon white truffle oil

2 tablespoons heavy cream

1 egg yolk

2 shallots, minced

1 red bell pepper, cored, ribs and seeds removed

2 medium carrots, peeled and cut lengthwise

2 medium leeks, sliced

2 celery hearts, sliced lengthwise

2 cups dry white wine

1 cup fish stock

2 tablespoons clam juice

1 medium tomato rose

Salt and pepper

Clean the fillets under cold running water. Pat dry with paper towels and set aside.

Melt 2 tablespoons butter in a large skillet until it foams. Stir in the flour and cook for a few moments; do not brown. Add the fish stock, blend well, and cook for 10 minutes, stirring constantly. Add the cream and continue to cook and stir until the sauce is smooth and well blended. Remove the sauce from the heat, stir in the egg yolk, and season with salt and pepper to taste. Stir to blend.

Butter a large saucepan with a lid, arrange the fillets in it, and add the shallots, bell pepper, carrots, leeks, celery, wine, fish stock, and clam juice. Season with salt and pepper to taste. Cover the pan, bring the liquid to a boil, stir gently, lower the heat, and simmer for at least 6 minutes, or until the vegetables are tender. Remove the bell pepper and dice.

Drain the fillets and place them on warmed plates. Pour the sauce over them and garnish with the cooked vegetables. Garnish with the bell pepper and the tomato rose. Serves 4.

Wine pairings: Lagaria or Sterling Chardonnay.

see color plate 26

Tuna with Fresh Herbs

Tonno alle Erbette

1 large ripe tomato, diced

4 teaspoons extra-virgin olive oil, divided

1 tablespoon sherry wine vinegar

Juice of 1 lime

1 teaspoon minced fresh basil

1 teaspoon minced fresh tarragon

1 teaspoon minced fresh dill

1 teaspoon minced fresh coriander (cilantro)

¼ teaspoon cracked black peppercorns

4 6-ounce fresh tuna fillets

Salt

For garnish:

4 medium leeks, cut lengthwise in 4 stalks

1 medium tomato rose

In a small skillet bring to boil water enough to cover the vegetables add salt. Place the leek stalks in the water and cook for 3 minutes. Remove them and set aside for garnish.

In a small bowl, combine the tomato, 2 tablespoons olive oil, vinegar, lime juice, herbs, and black pepper and season with salt to taste. Whisk until emulsified. Set aside.

Season the fillets with salt to taste. In a large skillet, heat 2 tablespoons olive oil until hot but not smoking. Add the fillets and cook over medium heat for 2 minutes. Turn and cook about 3 minutes more, or until the outside is lightly browned and the inside is still pink.

Transfer the fillets to warmed plates and top with the tomato and herb mixture. Serves 4.

Wine pairings: Arneis Blange Ceretto; Geyser Peak Chardonnay.

Tuna with Olives and Gherkin Relish

Tonno al Centriolo e Olive

6 tablespoons walnut oil

¼ cup fresh lemon juice

3 tablespoons minced garlic

2 teaspoons fresh oregano

4 6-ounce fresh tuna fillets

Relish:

⅔ cup pitted, coarsely chopped green olives

⅔ cup pitted, coarsely chopped black Italian Gaeta olives

½ cup minced red onion

¼ cup minced fresh basil leaves

¼ cup peeled and diced small cucumber (gherkin)

2 tablespoons minced fresh mint

1 tablespoon minced garlic

3 tablespoons fresh lemon juice

1 tablespoon fresh lime juice

1 tablespoon grated lemon peel

1 tablespoon extra-virgin olive oil

Salt and pepper

20 half slices of cucumber peeled, for garnish

Whisk the walnut oil, lemon juice, garlic, and oregano in a glass or ceramic baking dish. Season to taste with salt and pepper. Add the tuna and turn to coat. Cover with plastic wrap and refrigerate for 4 hours, turning every hour.

Combine all the relish ingredients in a bowl. Season with salt and pepper to taste and toss a few times. Let stand for 1 hour at room temperture.

Heat the grill to medium-hot (or use a nonstick square grill pan). Grill the tuna until it is just opaque in the center, 4–5 minutes per side.

Transfer the tuna to warmed plates. Spoon the relish over the tuna and garnish each plate with cucumber slices. Serves 4.

Wine pairings: Lagaria, della Venezie, or La Famiglia di Mondavi Pinot Grigio.

see color plate 27

Yellowtail with Artichokes

Dentice con Carciofi

8 medium firm Jerusalem artichokes, with outer leaves completely green and unspotted

1 tablespoon lemon juice

½ tablespoon coarse salt

1 teaspoon minced fresh marjoram

8 tablespoons extra-virgin olive oil, divided

1 garlic clove, crushed

4 6-ounce fresh yellowtail fillets

2 tablespoons dry white wine

2 tablespoons chicken stock

Salt and pepper

Clean the Jerusalem artichokes and slice 6 of them; soak the slices in cold water with the lemon juice for 10 minutes. Remove and spread on paper towels to dry.

Bring a pan of water to a boil, add the coarse salt, and cook the 2 whole Jerusalem artichokes for 6 minutes. Drain and mince finely. Stir in the marjoram.

Heat 3 tablespoons olive oil over medium-high heat until hot but not smoking. Add the garlic and cook 5 minutes. Season with salt and pepper to taste.

Season the fillets with salt and pepper to taste. Heat 4 tablespoons olive oil in a large skillet over medium-high heat until hot but not smoking. Cook the fillets until they are lightly browned on both sides, about 3 minutes per side. Add the wine and stock and cook for another minute.

In a medium skillet heat the remaining olive oil over medium-high heat until hot but not smoking and brown the artichoke slices, about 3 minutes, stirring occasionally. Season with salt and pepper to taste.

Divide the chopped artichokes evenly among 4 warmed dinner plates. Place a fillet in the center of each plate and top with sliced artichokes. Serves 4.

Wine pairings: Santa Margherita Pinot Grigio; Robert Mondavi Fumé Blanc.

see color plate 28

Yellowtail with Fennel and Tomatoes

Dentice al Finocchio e Pomodoro

2 tablespoons extra-virgin olive oil

1 large fennel bulb, halved, cored, and thinly sliced

2 bay leaves

½ cup minced shallots

1 small carrot, peeled and sliced

1 rib celery, thinly sliced

½ cup chicken stock

1 cup chopped San Marzano tomatoes, drained

¼ cup dry white wine

1 teaspoon finely grated orange zest

Pinch of saffron, crumbled

¾ teaspoon red pepper flakes

2 tablespoons concentrated Italian tomato paste (in tube)

4 6-ounce fresh yellowtail fillets

Salt and pepper

In a large skillet, heat the olive oil until hot but not smoking. Add the fennel, bay leaves, shallots, carrot, and celery. Cover and cook over moderate heat, stirring occasionally, until softened, about 12 minutes. Uncover and cook, stirring occasionally, until the vegetables are lightly browned, another 5 minutes. Add the tomatoes, wine, orange zest, saffron, and red pepper flakes, and cook over high heat until the liquid has evaporated, 5–7 minutes. Add the tomato paste, chicken stock season with salt and pepper to taste, lower the heat, and simmer for 5 minutes.

Arrange the fillets in the sauce in a single layer and season with salt and pepper to taste. Cover and cook over moderate heat for 6–8 minutes. Remove the fish from the skillet and keep warm on a platter covered with foil.

Force the sauce through a fine-mesh sieve into a bowl. Place the fish on warmed dinner plates and spoon the sauce over it. Serves 4.

Wine pairings: Lagaria or Cosentino Chardonnay.

Grilled Yellowtail with Sun-dried Tomatoes

Dentice al Pomodori Secchi

½ cup canola oil

½ cup fresh basil leaves, plus 5 tablespoons minced

1 cup fresh parsley sprigs, plus 4 tablespoons minced

½ tablespoon kosher salt, plus 2 teaspoons, divided

2 teaspoons freshly ground black pepper, divided

4 7-ounce fresh yellowtail fillets

12 oil-packed sun-dried tomatoes, drained and minced

10 garlic cloves, crushed

4 tablespoons minced fresh Italian parsley

4 tablespoons extra-virgin olive oil, plus extra for drizzling

Juice of 2 lemons

Salt and pepper

Combine the canola oil, whole basil leaves, 1 cup parsley sprigs, ½ tablespoon kosher salt, and 1 teaspoon black pepper in a bowl. Season the fillets with salt and pepper to taste and place them in a glass or ceramic pan. Coat the fish with the marinade, cover with foil, and refrigerate for 3 hours.

In a mixer, combine the sun-dried tomatoes with the garlic, minced basil, 4 tablespoons minced parsley, salt and pepper to taste, and 4 tablespoons olive oil, and beat until a paste forms.

Heat the grill (or a nonstick square grill pan) to medium-hot. Remove the fillets from the pan and grill them 4 minutes. Turn the fillets and evenly coat with the tomato paste; grill for another 5 minutes.

Place the fillets on warmed plates. Drizzle with the lemon juice and olive oil. Serves 4.

Wine pairings: Santa Margherita; Robert Mondavi Chardonnay.

SEVEN

Malaysia, Belgium, and Turkey, 1973–1976

Experiences with Customs and Foods of These Regions

FERDIE: As a boy you heard the stories about Malaysia through children's books. Now you could see where these stories took place. You were going to Kuala Lumpur. How did you cope there?

NINO: During my adolescence in Italy, I read about Sandokan and the Bengal Tigers, written by Italian storyteller Emilio Salgari. Now I was going to live where those stories took place. It was unbelievable.

In the beginning I could not adapt to the high humidity. Furthermore, the customs were confusing because the population fell into different ethnicities. It was common in groups of people to hear languages from three ethnic groups: Malay, Chinese, and East Indian. Each group held fast to its religion, language, and customs.

Nowhere was this more apparent than on the streets of the capital city, Kuala Lumpur. Many Muslim Malay women covered everything but their face and hands in light beige-colored headscarves and billowing robes. At the same time, Chinese girls dared to bare arms and legs.

The religious mix was fascinating. Half of the population was Muslim, the rest, Buddhist, Taoist, Christian, and Hindu. While the country's official language was Malay, many learned English in school and, luckily for me, it was the language spoken by everyone.

The hotel's general manager, Wolfgang Brandstaetter, hired me to be the director of operations of the Merlin, an eight-hundred-room hotel. It was the premier hotel of Kuala Lumpur in those days. I also had to oversee the operations of sister hotels in Singapore, Penang, and Pattaya Beach in Thailand.

Nino sightseeing in Brussels, 1974. Nino Pernetti collection.

Nino at the Thai festival dinner for executives of the Merlin Hotel, Kuala Lumpur, 1973. Nino Pernetti collection.

This was the first time that I had worked in a country with multiple races and religions. In order to quickly familiarize myself with the local cultures, the different customs and rituals, I hired a historian to help me understand 150 years of British colonialism.

The hotel was the center of the city's social life. Its Olympic-sized swimming pool, the only one of this size in Kuala Lumpur, was breathtaking, with an elevated terrace where traditional snacks and continental sandwiches were served overlooking the thick, verdant vegetation and orchids of every shape and color, coupled with numerous parakeets flying from tree to tree. It was *the* gathering place for high Western society. The contrast of colors was startling.

The hotel had six restaurants, including an elegant Chinese restaurant that seated 350. I went most Sundays to enjoy the dim sum served from straw baskets. There was a supper club serving international cuisine and with live shows, mainly from Australia, that changed monthly. Also there was an Indian restaurant where the smell of rich spices was prevalent. I was fond of the Hindu specialties, particularly any dish with curry. There was also a French restaurant serving Alsatian specialties, as the chef was from Colmar, France. The ballroom had a capacity of one thousand. Countless weddings were held there for rich Chinese, Indian, and Malaysian families.

On numerous occasions I spent the entire evening watching the different traditions and ceremonies, as they were very visually entertaining, with traditional music, colors, food, decor, and rituals. The banquet manager would place a chair for me next to the band. I would eat the food and observe all phases of the evening.

On Sunday I saw wealthy Chinese families march past the hotel's entrance and saw a line of chauffeured vintage Rolls-Royces. In this part of the world, the sign of wealth and social status was a Rolls-Royce. There was a discothèque open from 9:00 p.m. to 4:00 a.m., with two bands comprising great Philippine musicians. They did not know how to read music but they certainly played great by ear. In the Scots Bar there were only Chinese waitresses because the uniform was the traditional Scottish kilt, and they were the only group in Kuala Lumpur that could wear a skirt above the knee. There was a cozy coffee shop, where the waitresses wore the typical long batik dresses. The hotel felt like the United Nations with such sartorial variety.

Nino at the opening of the hotel discothèque, Kuala Lumpur, 1973. Nino Pernetti collection.

Kuala Lumpur abounded in festivities due to the multiethnic population. There was the Hari Raya Puasa festival, marking the end of Ramadan with three days of joyful celebrations. The Hari Raya Haji festival marked the successful completion of the Haj [the pilgrimage to Mecca] with a four-day feast of cakes and sweets. The Chinese New Year in January was ushered in with dances, parades, and much good cheer. The Festival of Thaipusam, in late March, was one of the most dramatic Hindu festivals, during which devotees honored Lord Subramaniam. The Kota Beldames Baser was a huge gathering held in May and included a massive market, traditional ceremonies, ornately decorated horsemen, medicine men, and tribal handicrafts. There were the huge Batu Caves, Kuala Lumpur's best-known tourist attraction, used for Hindu festivals and pilgrimages. The caves also formed an intense backdrop to the long-established festival during which Hindus inflicted pain on themselves by piercing various parts of the body.

I had to learn quickly about all the culinary customs and traditions of the various ethnicities. Consider this: in a Muslim diet, pork is strictly forbidden, so the majority of Malay dishes tend to be of beef or chicken. However, beef is never eaten by Hindus, to whom the cow is sacred. Pork remains the favorite meat of the Chinese. The Malay curries make great use of the omnipresent coconut and seldom include the yogurt so much favored by the Indian cooks. To the Chinese the sweet and sour flavor takes preference over the curry. And so it goes. The blend of spices is endless, and cooks are always turning out exciting combinations. Malaysia combines the best of Eastern and Western cuisine, and this is largely due to the fact that it has been a melting pot of those cultures.

One time the labor union brought the hotel's management before the Labor Court because the union maintained that the food served to the staff was not up to their quality standards. Of course I disputed this. But they claimed that I could not understand the flavor of their food because I was a westerner. When my turn came to testify, I simply said that good food had no nationality and everyone would understand if it pleased the palate or not. Furthermore, somewhat sarcastically, I told the judge (who happened to be East Indian) that, if we went by ethnicity, a Chinese could not understand Hindu food, just as a westerner could not understand Malay food. To the astonishment of all in the court, the judge looked at his watch and said, "It is 11:45. Why don't we all go to the hotel and have lunch at the employees' cafeteria?"

I looked at my Chinese attorney, who arched his eyebrows and said, "Nino, you better be right."

I replied, "We have no problem." The judge left after lunch very pleased with the food. Case closed.

I ate at the staff cafeteria at least two times a week, not only to savor the quality and taste of the food but mainly because after lunch I would play a few games of Ping-Pong in the recreation room with the employees.

I took my first trip to visit the Merlin Hotel on the Island of Penang in a Fokker airplane, about an hour's

Welcoming customers to an Easter buffet, Merlin Hotel, Singapore, 1973. Nino Pernetti collection

flight. Penang, "the Pearl of the Orient," is just off the northwest coast of peninsular Malaysia, on the storied Straits of Malacca. Its strategic location on the East-West spice route enticed the British into colonizing it in 1786 and accounts for its polyglot population and cultural richness.

The hotel had 275 rooms, all located on the beach. The population here was predominantly Chinese. In fact, the city had more Chinese ambiance than either Singapore or Hong Kong. In its older neighborhoods you would think that the clock had stopped at least eighty years earlier. There was a great contrast with Kuala Lumpur.

For me all the prerequisites were there: the white sand; the emerald-colored water; and plenty of palms scattered on the beach. I would stay a couple of days, do my inspections, have meetings with the general manager and department heads, and return to Kuala Lumpur. I was next on route to Singapore and, while driving to the hotel, I saw that everything was immaculate, streets clean, creative landscaping out of a book, traffic very disciplined, with no honking and no running of red lights. This was a model city for everything.

The ethnicity of the population was different from mainland Malaysia. The majority were Chinese, with Malays, Indians, and Eurasians constituting significant minorities. English was the principal language. The sister Merlin Hotel was well manicured and the staff alert to every detail. The Merlin's Chinese management was well trained and prepared. You had to ask them to do something only once, and they would implement it in a perfect manner.

There was a train linking Singapore to Kuala Lumpur. I took it one time, finding the journey an intriguing experience. At each stop I would observe and study the different kinds of people, so frugal in their behavior, faces so full of worry. They appeared to speak several dialects and carried with them many bundles. Singapore's nightlife was quite active, different from that of Kuala Lumpur.

The other city I had to visit was Pattaya Beach in Thailand. This popular resort was on the north Gulf

Nino tasting a new drink, Pattaya Beach, 1973. Nino Pernetti collection.

coast of eastern Thailand, about 120 miles from the capital, Bangkok. It was most famous for its many bars and indoor-outdoor restaurants. It was Thailand's most-visited city after Bangkok.

The hotel was situated at the center of the beach strip. With hundreds of beer and go-go bars (so they called them), the town was mostly frequented by European tourists. On the streets you heard people speaking German, Italian, and French. There was never a quiet moment on the streets—people strolling, drinking, eating—it gave you the impression that you were at a fair. You had people serenading cobras. At every corner you had Muay Thai boxing matches aimed at the tourists.

One time I was awestruck by a cobra and a mongoose fighting each other, similar to cock fighting. I found myself in the first row, but as the fight progressed people pushed forward. At one moment I was just inches from the deadly snake. The cobra struck

Nino injured during a soccer game, Kuala Lumpur, 1973. Nino Pernetti collection.

several times toward the mongoose, and the mongoose just pulled its head back millimeters, just like the Greatest, Muhammad Ali, did in many of his boxing matches. Finally, the tired cobra lost its quick reflexes, and the mongoose jumped on its head and put its razor-sharp teeth into its cranium until the cobra succumbed.

As in Key West, Florida, the sunset in Pattaya Beach was spectacular, breathtaking. There was always something going on there. You were in Thailand so you knew good food was never far away. Wherever you turned there were restaurants, food carts, food courts, food markets, motorcycle sidecar hot dog vendors, meatball vendors, and fruit sellers, both mobile and stationary. There was even a roaming coffee vendor pedaling a tut tut [a typical bicycle cart].

I always dedicated a half day to deep-sea diving to admire the beautiful underwater world rich with corals, thousands of species of fish, and small dolphins swimming and playing in groups. One day I was invited to go watch a soccer game. I was filled with anticipation to see how the Thais played soccer. When we arrived I didn't see any stadium, just a huge, grassless, open field, and, to my surprise, the game was played with elephants. I was stunned. You felt as if you were experiencing an earthquake. At one point I was invited to ride an elephant . . . and play. I felt right with it so I went. If you think that bungee jumping gets your adrenaline going,

Nino playing soccer with Merlin Hotel staff, Kuala Lumpur, 1973. Nino Pernetti collection.

Nino receiving a farewell gift from the Merlin Hotel staff, Kuala Lumpur, 1973. Nino Pernetti collection.

just wait until you are at the center for your soccer team on an elephant!

A couple of times I took the train to Bangkok, a four-hour trip. I would stare out the window, mesmerized by the greenery and the colorful villages, and I understood why Thailand was called the "Land of the Reigning Calm."

FERDIE: Nino, as soon as you got used to the high humidity and the monsoons of Malaysia you got transferred again, this time to the Brussels Sheraton Hotel in Belgium. Brussels was known to have the best and most Michelin star restaurants per capita in the world. Furthermore, management had to be top-notch due to the highly demanding clientele. So the expectations of you were high.

NINO: I was excited to go back to Europe. The hotel was brand-new in the posh Place Rogier, the Manhattan of Brussels. Brussels had a wide variety of great seafood restaurants. Here you found the smell of waffles on a cold winter's day (which were delicious when you went to the movies; no popcorn mania there). There were many cafés and clubs that never closed, plus forests practically at your doorstep, colorful pheasants, truffles in autumn, and plenty of designer shops.

Ah, but the weather. Brussels was a dark, dismal, gray city for most of the year. In that respect, it was not a joyful place. It was always raining or about to rain. An umbrella was essential. In July and August, the sun was very sparse. In fact, in those few moments when the sun did come out, everyone rushed to the Bois de la Cambre, the most popular park in Brussels, took off their shirts, and lay on the grass to enjoy those little and valuable moments in the balmy sun. Nobody moved; everyone looked like a Roman statue.

Not all was gray in Brussels, though, because my cousin Ivan lived there with his family. He was stationed at NATO headquarters and was familiar with the country and customs. That made life easier for me. I was able to pursue my passion for tennis, playing at NATO's indoor courts with him and other NATO employees.

The cuisine was also famous: *moules-frites* [mussels and fries], oyster stews, hams, cheese, Belgian beer, and, of course, the exquisite chocolates and pralines. Belgians are the biggest chocolate eaters in the world, consuming twenty-five pounds per person each year. No wonder wherever you turned there was a chocolate shop.

Belgian chocolates are the best in Europe if not the world. Everything was accentuated or punctuated by chocolate. In Brussels you didn't end a dinner without a nice selection of chocolate goodies; in fact, it was customary when you visited a friend to bring a box of elegantly wrapped chocolates.

The Sheraton Hotel, where I worked as the food and beverage director, was the newest in Brussels, and very American in its mentality. The top three floors were apartments with fully equipped kitchens and were for families facing relocation to Brussels. Most countries had three ambassadors, one for the government and one for the CEEC [Committee of European Economic Cooperation] and one for NATO respectively. Therefore, there was a significant demand for temporary apartments.

The traffic of CEOs, country presidents, and diplomats through Brussels was astounding. The hotel apartments and rooms were always full. The hotel was heavily frequented by state dignitaries. Henry Kissinger held many conferences in the private banquet rooms, and so did the American vice president, Spiro Agnew.

One thing I particularly remember is the hotel's main restaurant, Les Comtes de Flanders [The Counts of Flanders], very chic, Cristofle silverware and crystal glasses. But there had to be a dog menu! Belgians were very dog friendly, and to bring a dog of a certain size to a restaurant was perfectly normal. We had plastic or ceramic plates of different colors and sizes for dog food. The customers ordered different items from this menu for their dogs. And the menu changed regularly, too. May I add that I became a dog food expert.

Papá Vittorio, Mamma Teresa, and sister Lucia visiting Nino in Brussels, 1973. Nino Pernetti collection.

Orders did not have to be repeated and were executed as if the staff had learned from the best manual. The kitchen was dishing out the best food I had ever tasted. And people in Brussels knew the meaning of eating well. But after fourteen months of good eating and plenty of movies (the constant rain makes moviegoing one of the most popular pastimes) I was ready for a change when the home office informed me that I was due for a transfer.

I was told my next assignment was the Bombay Sheraton Hotel. There was quite a contrast between Belgium and Bombay. But I was partially comforted because I had visited India during a stopover in New Delhi. I was familiar with Indian culture because of my stint in Kuala Lumpur, where there was a large Indian population. Furthermore, I loved Indian food. I was ready to go.

Nino at the Italian food festival, Brussels, 1974. Nino Pernetti collection.

Three days before departure I was summoned to the home office, which was located in Brussels, and was told that there had been a change of plans. They told me that, because of my experience in opening hotels under difficult conditions, they needed me in the soon-to-be-opened Istanbul Sheraton Hotel.

In November I arrived in Istanbul. I flagged down a taxi to take me to the hotel. The taxi driver did not speak English but he said "okay" when I asked him to take me to the Sheraton Hotel. After over an hour of driving around I asked him whether he knew where he was going. He gave me a curt nod as a "yes" but said "Hayer," which meant "no." I arrived at 1:00 p.m. to find the hotel construction in its finishing stages.

I was thankful that most of the hotel staff had worked abroad, mainly in Germany, so I could communicate with many of them in German. But I found it easy to learn the language and started to speak some Turkish.

Since the hotel was still under construction, I stayed at the Divan Hotel across Taksim Square. It was November, and while Istanbul had a beautiful summer, winter there was very harsh, with much rain and wind. In order to reach the Sheraton I had to cross the square, actually a park with no greenery whatsoever.

Since the hotel wouldn't open for three months, I had plenty of time to acquaint myself with the city. During the summer there were tulips everywhere. The hotel's logo was a tulip.

I would go often to the ancient Hippodrome Park with a book in hand and would sit and read on a bench surrounded by beautiful trees while the bountiful flowers perfumed the air. Little is left of that gigantic stadium, which once stood at the heart of the Byzantine city of Constantinople. It is thought that the stadium held up to 100,000 people. The site is now an elongated public garden. There are also two obelisks from ancient Egypt and Greece. Next to them, at the entrance, you see the ruins where once stood four enormous bronze horses. They were pillaged during the Fourth Crusade in 1200 by the manipulative doge of Venice, Enrico Dandolo, and taken to Venice and placed on top of St. Mark's.

FERDIE: Nino, what else enchanted you in this new assignment?

NINO: What particularly drew my attention were the many coffeehouses at a junction in the labyrinthine old shopping complex at the heart of the city's bazaar. Nothing can prepare you for the Grand Bazaar. Streets covered by painted vaults are lined with hundreds and hundreds of boothlike shops. It is said to have over 2,500 booths whose wares will tempt you and whose shopkeepers are relentless in their quest for a sale.

As the hotel was getting ready to open, the staff was finishing its training. Istanbul was a veritable symphony of Occident and Orient divided by the Bosporus Strait. It was the hub of the metropolis, with a maze of narrow winding lanes filled with funky cafes, soulful bars, continental restaurants, and historic cinemas. Here's where I mostly learned to speak Turkish, because in Istanbul movies were shown in Turkish with subtitles.

Not too far from the hotel was the Sirkeci train station, where all the trains to and from Europe started and finished. This includes the world-famous Orient

Express. The famous Pera Palas Hotel was built especially to receive the wealthy and often distinguished passengers of the "King of Trains and the Train of Kings." The hotel had changed very little, relying on the hazy mystique of yesteryear. Inside it still evoked images of romance and exotic distant destinations. With a twenty-dollar bill to the concierge I was able to see room 411, still intact and decorated with Agatha Christie's books from the period when she stayed there, 1924–1933.

Finally, the Istanbul Sheraton, with its breathtaking view of the Bosporus Strait, opened. Istanbul's high society flowed in to see this marvel and patronize the restaurant, Le Mangal, which was booked solid three months in advance. Quality restaurants in Istanbul were only in deluxe hotels at the time. The restaurant served a blend of French and Italian cuisine. Turks generally did not wear jackets and ties when they went to a restaurant, so Le Mangal, after losing substantial business because of its coat-and-tie policy, changed the policy.

The hotel also had the Sultan Supper Club, with live bands. Though the dining room was full, I never saw any local couples dancing; eating and enjoying the music was what they liked.

There were no major problems running the hotel as the Turks were hard working. Turkish food rated high by my standards, very tasty and diverse. But whenever I went out to eat, I patronized the traditional *lokanta*, an ordinary restaurant offering a variety of typical Turkish dishes often listed at the entrance on a menu board. Many of Turkey's staple dishes are Central Asian and were taken there by nomads as they spread westward. Most Turkish meals began with *mezes*, Turkish starters or appetizers, of which there are hundreds of kinds. They range from simple combinations such as plain white cheese with melon to elaborately stuffed vegetables. *Mezes* were served in all Turkish restaurants and were generally accompanied with raki, a liqueur flavored with aniseed and with water added, similar to Pernod and Ouzo. Eating on the streets was very much a part of life in Istanbul.

You could not go far without coming across a café, street stall, or peddler selling snacks. There was an enormous number of street vendors. In summer I especially enjoyed a yogurt-based drink or a crispy cucumber that they would quarter and then generously sprinkle with salt and other spices and then stick together with toothpicks. In winter at every corner you could find roasted chestnuts. During summer or winter the most common drink was tea (chai), which was normally served black in small tulip-shaped glasses. It was offered wherever you went—shops, banks, or offices.

If Turks drank too much liquor they would eat *iskembe*, a rich, buttery tripe soup, before going to bed, which was said to prevent a hangover. I experienced this firsthand. It did work.

Yet again I was transferred, this time to Caracas to a new adventure.

Nino with the food and beverage department heads, Sheraton Hotel, Istanbul, 1975. Nino Pernetti collection.

Farewell gift from General Manager Abbatangelo of the Sheraton Hotel, Istanbul, 1976. Nino Pernetti collection.

MEAT

Sirloin Steak with Gorgonzola Sauce

Tagliata di Manzo al Gorgonzola

1 cup crumbled Italian Gorgonzola

1 tablespoon extra-virgin olive oil

4 tablespoons unsalted butter

1 tablespoon minced fresh Italian parsley

1 teaspoon minced fresh rosemary, plus 1 tablespoon

¼ cup toasted walnuts, chopped (see recipe, page 32)

5 large garlic cloves, peeled

4 10-ounce top sirloin steaks

Salt and pepper

Combine the Gorgonzola, olive oil, butter, parsley, and 1 teaspoon rosemary in a medium bowl. Stir to blend well. Mix in the walnuts. Season with salt and pepper to taste. Transfer the mixture to a small bowl and refrigerate.

Combine the 1 tablespoon rosemary and the garlic in the bowl of a mini food processor or a blender, season with salt and pepper to taste, and blend until the mixture almost forms a paste.

Salt the steaks lightly and place them in a baking dish. Rub the garlic paste on both sides of each steak. Cover and let stand ½ hour at room temperature.

Heat the grill (or a nonstick square grill pan) to medium-hot. Grill the steaks about 7 minutes on each side for medium, 2 minutes longer if using a grill pan. Transfer the steaks to a platter and let stand for 5 minutes. Cut each steak in slices. Divide the slices among 4 warmed plates and top each portion with the cheese mixture. Serves 4.

Wine pairings: Bertani; Artesa Cabernet Sauvignon.

see color plate 29

Beef Tenderloin with Aromatic Herbs

Filetto di Manzo alle Erbe Aromatiche

2 pounds center-cut beef tenderloin

Extra-virgin olive oil, for brushing

3 tablespoons Modena balsamic vinegar

4 tablespoons extra-virgin olive oil

3 sprigs fresh rosemary, minced

1 teaspoon minced fresh oregano

¼ teaspoon red pepper flakes

½ cup Cabernet

Salt and pepper

1 tablespoon coarse salt

Preheat the oven to 375°F.

Season the tenderloin with salt and pepper to taste. Brush on both sides with olive oil. Heat a large ovenproof skillet until hot but not smoking and sear the tenderloin, turning once, for 4 minutes. Place the skillet in the oven and cook for 10 minutes for medium, turning twice.

While the meat is cooking, in a saucepan combine the vinegar, olive oil, rosemary, oregano, red pepper flakes, and Cabernet. Whisk over low heat for about 6 minutes.

Cut the tenderloin into 8 slices diagonally. Divide the slices among 4 warmed plates, baste with the sauce, and sprinkle with the coarse salt. Serves 4.

Wine pairings: Ruffino Brunello di Montalcino; Caymus Cabernet Sauvignon.

see color plate 30

Beef Tenderloin with Black Pepper Sauce

Filetto di Manzo al Pepe Nero

4 6-ounce center-cut beef tenderloins, 1½ inches thick, pounded slightly

2 tablespoons crushed black pepper, divided

¼ cup Italian grappa

2 tablespoons Cognac

2½ tablespoons dried porcini mushrooms

1 cup boiling water

1 tablespoon vegetable oil

2 tablespoons unsalted butter

¼ cup minced shallots

1 garlic clove, crushed

¾ cup heavy cream

Salt and pepper

Rub ½ teaspoon of the crushed black pepper into each side of the tenderloins. Place them in a shallow dish and sprinkle with the grappa. Cover with plastic wrap and set aside at room temperature for 2 hours, turning every ½ hour.

While the meat is marinating, in a small heat-proof bowl, cover the mushrooms with the boiling water. Set aside for 30 minutes.

Preheat the oven to 250°F.

Remove the mushrooms from the soaking liquid, reserving the liquid, and rinse well. Cut off any tough bits and mince. Strain the soaking liquid through a fine sieve lined with cheesecloth and reserve ½ cup.

In a large, heavy skillet, heat the oil and butter over high heat until hot but not smoking. Season the tenderloins with salt to taste and cook until browned, about 2 minutes per side. Remove from the heat and add the cognac to the pan (it might ignite). Transfer the tenderloins to a baking dish and bake for 8–10 minutes for medium.

While the meat is baking, add the shallots and garlic to the cognac, cover, and cook over moderate heat for about 6 minutes. Increase the heat to high, add the reserved half cup of mushroom soaking liquid, and cook, stirring constantly, until syrupy, about 2 minutes. Stir in the cream and cook until slightly reduced, 2 minutes. Stir in the mushrooms, reduce the heat to low, and cook 4 minutes longer. Season with salt to taste.

Transfer the tenderloins to warmed plates. Stir any meat juices into the sauce and spoon over tenderloins. Serves 4.

Wine pairings: Einaudi Barolo; Caymus Cabernet Sauvignon.

Salt-baked Beef Tenderloin

Filetto di Manzo al Sale

3 pounds coarse salt

5 garlic cloves, minced

3 sprigs fresh rosemary, minced

2 pounds center-cut beef tenderloin

4 tablespoons rosemary-flavored olive oil (place 2–3 rosemary sprigs in a bottle of olive oil for 4 days), divided

1 tablespoon dried oregano

4 large ripe tomatoes

Salt and pepper

Preheat the oven to 400°F.

On a baking tray layer half the coarse salt and scatter the garlic and rosemary evenly over it. Lay the tenderloin on the salt. Cover the meat completely with the rest of the salt. Cook for 30 minutes for medium.

Remove the tray from the oven and smash the salt crust with the back of a serving spoon; it will break in half. Place the tenderloin in a large, heavy skillet with 1 tablespoon of the olive oil, turn twice, then season with salt and pepper to taste and ½ of the oregano. Remove the tenderloin from the skillet and set aside.

Slice the tomatoes into 8 equal slices, sprinkle with remaining oregano, and season with salt and pepper to taste. Pour the remaining oil over the meat. Place 2 tomato slices on each plate. Cut the tenderloin into 8 slices and place a slice on each tomato slice. Serves 4.

Wine pairings: Bertani Amarone; Charles Krug Meritage.

Lamb Tenderloins with Marsala

Filettini d'Agnello al Marsala

4 tablespoons extra-virgin olive oil

3 garlic cloves, minced

2 teaspoons minced fresh rosemary

8 3-ounce lamb tenderloins, pounded slightly

2 cups beef stock

1 cup Cabernet

1 cup sweet Marsala

2 tablespoons Italian Grappa

3 tablespoons Champagne mustard

4 tablespoons unsalted butter

Salt and pepper

In a glass or ceramic bowl whisk the olive oil, garlic, and rosemary. Season with salt and pepper to taste. Add the lamb tenderloins and turn to coat evenly. Let stand 2 hours at room temperature, turning every half hour. Remove the lamb from the marinade.

In a heavy, medium saucepan bring the stock, Cabernet, and Marsala to a boil, reduce the heat, and cook until reduced, about 25 minutes.

Heat a heavy, large skillet on high heat until hot but not smoking. Add ½ tablespoon olive oil and sear the tenderloins 1 minute on each side. Once the loins are seared remove the grease and flame them with the Grappa. Be careful it may ignite. Reduce the heat to medium-high and cook the tenderloins for 5 minutes, turning once, for medium rare. Remove the meat to a platter and cover with foil.

Pour the wine sauce into the skillet and bring to a boil, scraping up any browned bits. Remove the skillet from the heat and whisk in the mustard. Add the butter and whisk until it melts. Season with salt and pepper to taste.

Cut each lamb tenderloin into 4 slices. Add any meat juice to the Marsala sauce. Place 2 slices of meat on each warmed plate, stir the sauce, and pour it over each serving. Serves 4.

Wine pairings: Einaudi Barbera; Joseph Phelps Cabernet Sauvignon.

Lamb Chops with Dried Cherries and Berries

Costolette d'Agnello alle Ciliege e Mirtilli Secchi

11 tablespoons extra-virgin olive oil, divided

1¾ cup Cabernet, divided

1 tablespoon minced fresh thyme, plus 1 teaspoon

16 2-ounce lamb chops, pounded slightly

½ cup mixed dried cherries and berries, plus 2 tablespoons for garnish

4 medium shallots, thinly sliced

1½ cup shiitake mushrooms, stems discarded, caps thinly sliced

1½ cups beef stock

½ tablespoon honey

2 tablespoons minced fresh Italian parsley

Arugula, for garnish

Salt and pepper

In a glass or ceramic bowl whisk 4 tablespoons olive oil with 1 tablespoon Cabernet and 1 tablespoon thyme and season with salt and pepper to taste. Pour the marinade over the lamb chops and refrigerate for 5 hours, turning occasionally. Soak the cherries and berries in 1 cup Cabernet for 1 hour; drain.

In a saucepan, heat 2 tablespoons olive oil until hot but not smoking. Add the shallots and mushrooms and cook over moderately high heat about 2 minutes. Add the stock, 1 teaspoon thyme, and the remaining wine to the saucepan and bring to a boil over high heat. Boil until partially reduced, about 4 minutes. Add the honey, parsley, and drained fruit. Lower the heat and cook for 3 minutes. Strain the sauce through a fine-mesh sieve, pressing on the solids with a wooden spoon.

Remove the chops from the marinade and pat them dry with paper towels. Season with salt to taste. In a large skillet, heat the remaining oil over high heat until hot but not smoking. Add the chops and cook about 4 minutes a side for rare. Remove the chops from the skillet and drain the oil from the skillet. Pour the sauce into the skillet and cook over high heat, scraping the bottom of the pan, until reduced slightly, about 2 minutes. Season with salt and pepper to taste.

To serve, divide the sauce evenly among 4 warmed plates, reserving some for garnish. Place 4 chops on each plate. Dot each chop with sauce and garnish with a berry and arugula. Serves 4.

Wine pairings: Altesino Brunello di Montalcino; Charles Krug Meritage.

see color plate 31

Pork Tenderloins with Applesauce

Filetti di Maiale con Salsa Mele

3 large Granny Smith apples, peeled, cored, and thinly sliced

¼ cup dry Marsala

1 tablespoon Calvados

½ cup water

1 small slice fresh ginger, peeled

½ cinnamon stick

2½ tablespoons unsalted butter, divided

1 tablespoon bread crumbs

1 tablespoon light-brown sugar

1 tablespoon extra-virgin olive oil

8 3-ounce center-cut pork tenderloins, slightly pounded

2 rosemary sprigs

Salt and pepper

In a large skillet, combine the apples, Marsala, Calvados, water, ginger, cinnamon stick, and 1 tablespoon of butter. Bring to a simmer, cover, and cook over moderately low heat, stirring occasionally, about 14 minutes. Uncover and cook another 5 minutes, stirring until the liquid is almost evaporated. Discard the ginger and cinnamon stick. Stir in the bread crumbs with the light brown sugar and simmer a few more minutes. Scoop the apple pulp into a food processor or blender and purée until small chunks remain. Transfer the apple purée to a small bowl, cover, and keep warm.

In a large skillet, heat the olive oil until shimmering. Season the pork tenderloins with salt and pepper to taste. Cook over high heat, turning once, until browned on both sides, about 8 minutes for medium rare. Transfer the pork to a plate and keep warm.

Return the skillet to high heat and add the remaining butter and the rosemary. Cook, stirring, until the rosemary browns, 2–3 minutes. Discard the rosemary.

Divide the applesauce evenly among 4 warmed plates; place the pork tenderloins alongside it. Spoon the rosemary butter over the meat. Serves 4.

Wine pairings: Ruffino Ducale Tan Label Chianti Classico; Joseph Phelps Merlot.

Pork Tenderloins with Balsamic-Plum Sauce

Filetti di Maiale con Salsa alle Prugne e Balsamico

½ cup dried plums, pitted and quartered

1 cup Cabernet

1 tablespoon light-brown sugar

3 tablespoons Modena balsamic vinegar

¾ cup beef stock

2 tablespoons olive oil

2 1-pound pork tenderloins

½ medium onion, minced

4 shallots, minced

1 garlic clove, minced

2 tablespoons unsalted butter

1 tablespoon minced fresh rosemary

Salt and pepper

Place the dried plums and Cabernet in a ceramic bowl and let stand overnight, stirring a few times. Transfer the fruit and soaking liquid to a saucepan. Add the brown sugar and balsamic vinegar and boil over high heat until the liquid is reduced, about 8 minutes. Add half of the stock to the plums and continue to boil until the mixture is reduced by half, stirring occasionally. Set aside.

Preheat the oven to 450°F. Heat the olive oil in a heavy, large oven-proof skillet over medium-high heat until the oil is hot but not smoking. Sear the tenderloins 2–3 minutes, turning once. Add the onion and shallots and continue cooking until the tenderloins are brown on all sides and the onion is translucent, about 6 minutes. Add the garlic. Place the skillet in the oven and cook the pork 4–5 minutes.

Transfer the pork to a platter and tent with foil to keep warm. Add the remaining stock to the skillet and cook, scraping up any browned bits, until the liquid is nearly evaporated, about 3 minutes. Stir in the butter and the plum mixture and cook for 2 minutes, stirring frequently. Force the mixture through a fine-mesh sieve with a wooden spoon.

Cut the tenderloins into 8 slices and divide them among 4 warmed plates. Pour sauce over each tenderloin and garnish with rosemary. Serves 4.

Wine pairings: Ruffino Brunello di Montalcino; Artesa Cabernet Sauvignon.

see color plate 32

Pork Tenderloins with Wild Mushrooms

Filetti di Maiale con Funghi di Bosco

1 cup dried mixed mushrooms, chopped

8 3-ounce center-cut pork loins, slightly pounded

All-purpose flour, for dredging

2 large eggs, beaten

3 cups fresh bread crumbs, seasoned with salt, pepper, pinch of nutmeg, ½ tablespoon dried parsley flakes, ½ teaspoon dried oregano

3 tablespoons extra-virgin olive oil

4 tablespoons unsalted butter

2 tablespoons minced garlic

1 bay leaf

¾ cup dry white wine

¾ cup beef stock

1 cup chopped canned tomatoes

1 tablespoon fresh minced rosemary

Salt and pepper

Soak the mushrooms in water to cover for 30 minutes. Drain, reserving 1 tablespoon soaking liquid.

Season the pork tenderloins with salt and pepper to taste. Dredge in flour, then in the beaten eggs, then in the bread crumbs, coating completely. Heat the olive oil in a heavy, large skillet over medium-high heat until hot but not smoking. Sauté the pork tenderloins until just cooked through, about 3 minutes per side for medium rare. Transfer the meat to a platter and cover with foil to keep warm.

Wipe out the skillet with paper towels. In the same skillet, melt the butter over medium-high heat until it foams. Add the garlic and sauté 1 minute. Add the chopped mushrooms and cook 3 minutes. Add the bay leaf, wine, stock, and tomatoes and bring to a boil; boil until thick, 6–8 minutes. Remove the bay leaf and stir in the rosemary and 1 tablespoon of mushroom soaking liquid. Season the sauce with salt and pepper to taste.

Divide the sliced pork tenderloins among 4 warmed plates and pour the sauce over it. Serves 4.

Wine pairings: Felsina Chianti Classico; Franciscan Oakville Estate Cabernet Sauvignon.

Veal Chops with Grapes and Marsala

Costolette di Vitello all'Uva e Marsala

1 pound seedless red grapes, halved

3 tablespoons Modena balsamic vinegar

2 tablespoons sweet Marsala

2 tablespoons unsalted butter, plus 1 tablespoon, softened

2 tablespoons beef stock

2 tablespoons extra-virgin olive oil

4 14-ounce veal loin chops

All-purpose flour, for dredging

4 medium tomatoes to make rose flowers

Arugula, for garnish

Salt and pepper

Preheat the oven to 475°F.

On a baking sheet, toss the grapes with the vinegar, Marsala, and the tablespoon of softened butter; season with salt and pepper to taste. Roast for 10–12 minutes, shaking the baking sheet halfway through. Remove the baking sheet from the oven, transfer the grapes to a bowl, and keep warm. Pour the stock into the baking sheet and stir to scrape up any browned bits. Pour the stock in a bowl and keep warm. Reduce the oven temperature to 375°F.

In a 12-inch ovenproof skillet, heat 2 tablespoons butter and the olive oil over medium-high heat until the butter is completely melted. Dredge the chops in flour and add to the skillet. Cook for 4 minutes, or until brown, turning once. Season with salt and pepper to taste. Place the skillet in the oven and bake the chops for 15 minutes for medium. Remove the skillet from the oven.

Combine the grapes and the stock mixture. Season with salt and pepper to taste.

Divide the chops among 4 warmed plates and top with the grape-and-stock mixture. Garnish with tomato roses and arugula. Serves 4.

Wine pairings: Ruffino Riserva Ducale Gold Label Chianti Classico; Charles Krug Meritage

see color plate 33

The Making of Veal Scaloppine

It is important to buy good-quality veal because it cooks so quickly. Buy the palest pink meat you can find in the market; if it is dark pink or reddish, it will tend to be tough.

Do not overcook veal. Never dredge the scaloppini in flour until you are ready to cook them; if you do it ahead of time, the flour becomes damp, and the meat does not brown properly. Make sure the oil and butter are very hot when you put the scaloppine in the pan.

To cook veal scaloppine, heat 1 tablespoon olive oil and ½ tablespoon butter in a large skillet over medium heat. When the butter is completely melted, add as many freshly dredged scaloppine as will fit in the pan without touching. Season with salt and pepper to taste. Cook them very quickly, until the edges are lightly browned. Remove the scaloppine from the pan to a warm plate and cover with foil to keep warm. Pour off all the fat from the skillet and return the skillet to the heat to deglaze the pan. Proceed to make the sauce of your choice.

When the sauce is finished, return the scaloppine to the pan, tucking them into the sauce. Cook, turning the scaloppine in the sauce, until they are heated through and the sauce is slightly thickened. If necessary, add a bit of chicken stock if the sauce is too thick.

Veal Scaloppine with Fontina

Scaloppine con Fontina

4 tablespoons extra-virgin olive oil, divided

2 tablespoons unsalted butter, divided

All-purpose flour, for dredging

8 3-ounce scaloppine, ¼-inch thick, pounded to ⅛ inch

2 tablespoons of chicken stock

½ cup white dry wine

1 cup diced Italian fontina

2 teaspoons white truffle oil

Salt and pepper

Heat 1 tablespoon olive oil and ½ tablespoon butter in a large skillet over medium heat. Dredge the scaloppine in flour. When the butter is completely melted, put as many scaloppine in the pan as will fit without touching. Sauté for 2 minutes on each side. Season with salt and pepper to taste. Remove the scaloppine from the pan to a warm plate and cover with aluminum foil to keep warm. Pour off all the fat from the skillet and return the skillet to the heat to deglaze. Add the stock to the skillet, scraping up any browned bits from the bottom of the skillet.

In a small saucepan melt the remaining butter in the wine. Add the fontina and the truffle oil and cook over low heat, stirring, until the sauce is piping hot and the cheese melts, and pour it into the skillet. Divide the scaloppine among 4 warmed dinner plates and spoon the sauce over. Serves 4.

Wine pairings: Travaglini Gattinara; Estancia Estates Pinot Noir.

Veal Scaloppine Pizzaiola

Scaloppine alla Pizzaiola

4 tablespoons extra-virgin olive oil, divided

3 tablespoons unsalted butter, divided

All-purpose flour, for dredging

8 3-ounce scaloppine, ¼-inch thick, pounded to ⅛ inch

2 tablespoons chicken stock

4 garlic cloves, sliced

½ tablespoon minced fresh oregano

1 teaspoon dried oregano

½ cup tomato sauce (see recipe, page 61), heated

1 tablespoon concentrated Italian tomato paste (in tube)

2 tablespoons Cabernet

1 tablespoon imported capers, drained

1 tablespoon minced fresh Italian parsley

Salt and pepper

Heat 1 tablespoon olive oil and ½ tablespoon butter in a large skillet over medium heat. Dredge the scaloppine in flour. When the butter is completely melted, put as many scaloppine in the pan as will fit without touching. Sauté for 2 minutes on each side. Season with salt and pepper to taste. Remove the scaloppine from the pan to a warm plate and cover with foil to keep warm. Pour all the fat from the skillet and return the skillet to the heat to deglaze. Add 1 tablespoon chicken stock to the skillet, scraping up any browned bits from the bottom of the skillet. Reserve liquid.

Pour the remaining olive oil into the skillet. Stir in the garlic and sauté briefly. Add the fresh and dried oregano, the warm tomato sauce, the tomato paste, Cabernet. Add the remaining chicken stock and capers. Stir a few times and season with salt and pepper to taste. Simmer uncovered for 6–8 minutes to reduce the mixture to a thick sauce. Place the scaloppine into the pan and spoon a little sauce over them. Reduce the heat, cover, and simmer for 5 minutes, turning a few times.

Divide the scaloppine evenly among 4 warmed plates, top with sauce, and garnish with parsley. Serves 4.

Wine pairings: Villa Antinori Red Zinfandel; Charles Krug.

Veal Scaloppine with Prosciutto and Arugula

Scaloppine con Prosciutto e Arugula

6 tablespoons extra-virgin olive oil, divided

⅔ cup thinly julienned Italian prosciutto

2 large garlic cloves, minced

2 tablespoons unsalted butter

All-purpose flour, for dredging

8 3-ounce scaloppine, ¼-inch thick, pounded to ⅛ inch

2 tablespoons Modena balsamic vinegar

1 tablespoon chicken stock

1 pound arugula, leaves only, minced, plus more for garnish

2 cups minced, drained canned tomatoes

Salt and pepper

In a skillet, heat 2 tablespoons olive oil over moderate heat, until hot but not smoking. Add the prosciutto and garlic and cook, stirring, until the garlic is golden, about 5 minutes. Transfer to a plate.

Heat 1 tablespoon olive oil and ½ tablespoon butter in a large skillet over medium heat. Dredge the scaloppine in flour. When the butter is completely melted, put as many scaloppine in the pan as will fit without touching. Sauté for 2 minutes on each side. Season with salt and pepper to taste. Remove the scaloppine from the pan to a warm plate and cover with aluminum foil to keep warm. Pour all the fat from the skillet and return the skillet to the heat. Add the balsamic vinegar and stock to the skillet and cook, scraping up any browned bits, until the liquid is nearly evaporated. Add the arugula and toss until wilted, about 2 minutes. Add the tomatoes and prosciutto and cook over high heat for 2 minutes, stirring occasionally; season with salt and pepper to taste.

Divide the scaloppine evenly among 4 warmed plates and top with the sauce. Garnish with arugula. Serves 4.

Wine pairings: Travaglini Gattinara; Clos du Bois Merlot.

see color plate 34

Veal Scaloppine with Sage and Lemon

Scaloppine alla Salvia e Limone

7 tablespoons extra-virgin olive oil, divided

2 tablespoons unsalted butter

All-purpose flour, for dredging

8 3-ounce scaloppine, ¼-inch thick, pounded to ⅛ inch

8 slices lemon

½ cup chicken stock

¼ cup fresh lemon juice

½ teaspoon minced fresh Italian parsley

24 large fresh sage leaves

1 cup vegetable oil, for deep frying

Salt and pepper

Preheat the oven to 200°F.

Heat 1 tablespoon olive oil and ½ tablespoon butter in a large skillet over medium heat. Dredge the scaloppine in flour. When the butter is completely melted, put as many scaloppine in the pan as will fit without touching. Sauté for 2 minutes on each side. Season with salt and pepper to taste. Remove the scaloppine from the pan and overlap on a warm plate with a slice of lemon on each scaloppine; keep warm in the oven covered with foil. Pour all the fat from the skillet and return the skillet to the heat. Add the chicken stock and bring to a boil, scraping up all the brown bits. Add the lemon juice, season with salt and pepper to taste, and boil for another minute or so. Remove the skillet from the heat, add the remaining butter, and whisk until blended. Stir in the parsley.

Heat the vegetable oil in a medium skillet until hot but not smoking. Add the sage leaves and fry until the sizzling subsides, about 1 minute. Using a slotted spoon, transfer the sage to paper towels to drain.

Remove the scaloppine from the oven and divide evenly among 4 warmed plates. Discard the lemon slices. Top each plate with some of the lemon sauce and 4 fried sage leaves. Serves 4.

Wine pairings: Friuli-Venezia Giulia Sauvignon Collio; Chateau Montelena, Chardonnay.

Veal Scaloppine with Cream-Mustard Sauce

Scaloppine alla Crema e Mostarda

4 tablespoon extra-virgin olive oil, divided

2 tablespoons unsalted butter, divided

All-purpose flour, for dredging

8 3-ounce scaloppine, ¼-inch thick, pounded to ⅛ inch

5 tablespoons minced shallots

⅔ cup chicken stock, divided

2 tablespoons dry Marsala

2 tablespoons minced fresh sage, divided

4 teaspoons French Champagne mustard

½ cup cream

Salt and pepper

Heat 1 tablespoon olive oil and ½ tablespoon butter in a large skillet over medium heat. Dredge the scaloppine in flour. When the butter is completely melted, put as many scaloppine in the pan as will fit without touching. Sauté for 2 minutes on each side. Season with salt and pepper to taste. Remove the scaloppine from the pan to a warm plate and cover with aluminum foil to keep warm. Pour all the fat from the skillet and return the skillet to the heat to deglaze. Pour 1 tablespoon chicken stock into the skillet, scraping up any browned bits from the bottom of the skillet.

Add the shallots to the same skillet and cook, stirring 1 minute. Add the remaining stock, Marsala, 1 tablespoon sage, and the mustard; cook until very thick, scraping up any browned bits, about 4 minutes. Add the cream and cook until the sauce thickens, about 1 minute. Mix in the remaining sage and any meat juices. Season with salt and pepper to taste.

Divide the scaloppine evenly among 4 warmed plates and top with the sauce. Serves 4.

Wine pairings: Travaglini Gattinara; Estancia Estates Pinot Noir.

Sweet-and-Sour Veal Scaloppine

Scaloppine in Agrodolce

4 tablespoons extra-virgin olive oil, divided

2½ tablespoons unsalted butter, divided

1 medium onion, minced

1 garlic clove, minced

6 fresh basil leaves, minced

3 bell peppers, 1 each red, green, yellow, ½-inch dice

1 pound canned tomatoes, drained

2 tablespoons red wine vinegar

2 teaspoons light-brown sugar

8 3-ounce scaloppine, ¼-inch thick, pounded to ⅛ inch

All-purpose flour for dredging

1 tablespoon minced Italian parsley

Salt and pepper

Heat 3 tablespoons olive oil and 2 tablespoons butter in a skillet until the butter melts. Stir in the onion, garlic, and basil and cook for 2 minutes. Add the bell pepper and cook for 10 minutes. Add the tomatoes and season with salt and pepper to taste. Stir in the vinegar and brown sugar. Cover and cook for 25 minutes, stirring occasionally.

Preheat the oven to 350°F. Heat 1 tablespoon olive oil and ½ tablespoon butter in a large skillet over medium heat. Dredge the scaloppine in flour. When the butter is completely melted, put as many scaloppine in the pan as will fit without touching. Sauté for 2 minutes on each side. Transfer the scaloppine to a ceramic dish and distribute the bell pepper mixture evenly over the meat. Bake for 6 minutes.

Divide the scaloppine evenly among 4 warmed plates. Top each serving with sauce and garnish with parsley. Serves 4.

Wine pairings: Brolio Chianti Classico; Clos du Bois Merlot.

Veal Tenderloins with Mushrooms

Filettini di Vitello ai Funghetti

4 tablespoons unsalted butter, divided

2 shallots, minced

½ cup Cabernet

1 teaspoon cracked black peppercorns

1 teaspoon minced fresh thyme

1 cup beef stock

⅓ cup finely cubed beef marrow

2 tablespoons extra-virgin olive oil

8 button mushroom caps, sliced

½ cup dry Marsala

Juice of ½ lemon

1 bay leaf

8 3-ounce veal tenderloins, pounded slightly

All-purpose flour, for dredging

½ tablespoon grappa

2 red bell peppers, roasted and diced (see recipe, page 36)

Salt and pepper

Melt 2 tablespoons butter in a skillet on medium-high heat. Sauté the shallots for 1 minute. Add the Cabernet, peppercorns, and thyme and reduce by one-third. Add the stock and cook for about 17 minutes. Add the marrow and cook for 10 minutes more. Skim off the grease, remove the skillet from the heat, and, with a wooden spoon, force the mixture through a fine sieve until the beef marrow dissolves completely. Set aside.

In a small skillet heat the olive oil over medium-high heat until hot but not smoking. Brown the mushrooms for 2 minutes. Add the Marsala, lemon juice, and bay leaf and season with salt and pepper to taste. Cook for 3 minutes. Remove the bay leaf.

In a large skillet heat the remaining butter until it foams. Dredge the tenderloins in flour and cook for 10 minutes, turning once, over medium-low heat. Remove the tenderloins from the skillet and keep them warm. Wipe out the skillet with a paper towel. Add the grappa (it may ignite). Stir in the mushroom sauce and cook for 3 minutes, to reduce slightly. Force the sauce through a fine sieve. Pour the sauce evenly among 4 warmed plates. Place 2 tenderloins on each plate and garnish with the diced bell peppers. Serves 4.

Wine pairings: Villa Antinori; Francis Coppola Claret.

see color plate 35

EIGHT

Caracas to Paris, 1976–1982

Appreciation of Venezuelan and French Cuisine

FERDIE: Nino, you went home to Italy before embarking to the Americas and while you were there you went to the Venezuelan Consulate in Milan to pick up your work visa. You've told me that, while sitting in the waiting room, you were puzzled to see framed newspapers dated 1950. They were ads for jobs in Venezuela, no matter what skills the applicant had. A clerk told you that many Italians took the offer. You were happy to learn that the Italian community was strongly represented in Caracas. How did you like your time there?

Nino in front of the Eiffel Tower, Paris, 1981. Nino Pernetti collection.

NINO: I arrived there at night. While driving from the airport to Caracas I saw only glittering lights resembling San Francisco. It was at that time a land of contrasts, not at all a nice view during the day. Be that as it may, from afar we could see the hotel on the hill, a majestic presence and architectural splendor. I was going to the 650-room Tamanaco Hotel, with five restaurants, three bars, one nightclub, and banquet rooms to accommodate up to 2,500 people. It had a 500-seat tennis stadium with a small snack bar for the players and fans. It was the number one hotel profit-maker in the entire Inter-Continental chain.

The pressure was on, as I knew I was going to be received with high expectations, and I don't mind telling you my heart pounded in anticipation. I was going to be the director of food and beverage, with 400 employees in my department.

When I walked into the ornate lobby at 10:00 p.m., I was welcomed by the Belgian general manager, Jacques Duwelz. The lobby was huge and from its traffic looked like New York's Grand Central Station. The oil fields had been nationalized, so the country was booming. Everyone was spending money. The restaurants were always filled with people from all walks of life—plenty of Dom Perignon and Chivas Regal. Venezuela at that time was per capita the world's largest importer of Scotch whisky, and second only to France in per capita premium-champagne drinkers. European- and American-based airlines were flying daily to Caracas, as were jumbo jets and the Concorde.

I remember that a real estate company out of Miami rented one of the private banquet rooms for six months at a time. It was making sales pitches to the Venezuelans to purchase houses and apartments in Miami and throughout Florida. There were ten small tables set up for sales people, a lot of photos and papers. They entertained potential buyers with lunch and dinner and then showed them slides of their future house or apartment. They were selling homes in bundles.

At that time there were cruise ships coming into Caracas, and part of their tour was to have lunch at the Tamanaco. There would be a crowd of a thousand to fifteen hundred at a time. On sunny days we would prepare the terraces to accommodate the tourists. The Tamanaco was also a tourist attraction, because it stood on a hill, and the view of the city was spectacular.

Many well-to-do Venezuelans had their own single-engine airplanes. Caracas's La Carlota Airport was the busiest small-aircraft landing field in the world. It could be seen from the Tamanaco, since it was just down the hill.

The hotel was buzzing around the clock. There was a 105 percent occupancy year around; almost daily we had to rent the pool cabanas because many businessmen arrived without reservations, and there were no other hotel rooms available in Caracas.

Nino speaking at the InterContinental Hotel conference, Caracas, 1976. Nino Pernetti collection.

Nino teaching at a seminar workshop in Caracas, 1977. Nino Pernetti collection.

The first change I made was to open the coffee shop earlier than 5:00 a.m. Caracas's nightclubs and discotheques were open until the early hours. Many times, before five o'clock there were lines of people coming to eat breakfast . . . or to get a bite before going to sleep. Within a few weeks news spread that we had started to open at 4:00 a.m. to serve a minibreakfast buffet. I found Venezuelan breakfast in all its regional permutations endlessly seductive. I included on the menu the national dish, *pabellón criollo* (shredded beef with peppers) and *carne mechada* (stuffed roast beef) along with *arroz blanco* (white rice), *caraotas negras* (black beans) sprinkled with grated aged cow's milk cheese, and strips of fried *plátanos* (plantains). These were working-class staples, with the beef usually enlivened with onions, tomatoes, garlic, and green peppers. There was sugar to be sprinkled on the black beans for those who liked them sweet. There was always a nice tray of doughnut-shaped fried *arepas*, which are crunchy patties made from ground cracked white corn. Another version of *arepas*, made from wheat flour and resembling pita bread, was eaten with *nata* (the Venezuelan crème fraîche) as a spread. Egg dishes were made with *queso blanco* (white cheese), a cheese resembling Italian mozzarella. Scrambled eggs were laced with cilantro and minced onions and tomatoes and served with piping-hot *arepas*.

Two waitresses wearing typical native Andean dress made *cachapas* (ground sweet-corn pancakes) behind the buffet, filling them with a slice of a regional cheese called *queso guayanés*. This cheese contrasted well with the pancakes' slightly sweet flavor. Of course, there was the ever-popular cake *bienmesabe*, which means "tastes good to me." This was a sponge cake dressed in coconut cream finery. Completing the buffet was a soup called *pisca andina*, made of boiled potatoes in a milky broth seasoned with cilantro and garnished with a julienne of cucumbers and cubes of fresh cheese.

There was also a coffee station. Venezuelans' love for their coffee is justified. It is scrumptious. Always sticklers for things they consider important, Venezuelans have devised a vocabulary to define exactly how they like their coffee: *guayoyo* (black and weak, American style, served in an espresso cup), *negro* (black and deadly), *marrón obscuro* or *marrón claro* (dark or light brown), *cortadito* (a mini cappuccino), and *con leche* (with milk). Of course, there was hot chocolate. Venezuela produces some of the world's best cacao.

At that time, with such a young population, many with money to burn, Caracas's nightlife hopped all week long and not just on the weekends. Nightspots changed as fast as people changed their shirts. In Caracas the "in" crowd constantly sought new places to be seen sipping their favorite whisky or champagne. Parties started at midnight, so in no time the idea of the breakfast buffet became the talk of the town. Additionally, I made arrangements with the most popular discotheque to include as part of their cover charge a reduced price for the Tamanaco's breakfast buffet. It was a win-win situation for both of us. Venevisión, the most popular TV station, filmed this early morning buffet and featured it many times in their broadcast.

One February day my friend Camillo Coppola, knowing I liked scuba diving, asked if I would join him and a group of friends to sail on his yacht to Los Roques

From right to left: Nino, *Mission Impossible's* Greg Morris, Gary Mason, and Manolo Olalguiaga at the Tamanaco Hotel, Caracas, 1979. Nino Pernetti collection.

Islands for the weekend. I had never been there and had heard of the islands' attractiveness. It was a four-hour trip and a giant leap into an incredible marine world. Beneath the emerald waters were walls of corals and fish of all kinds, sponges and anemones, providing everyone excellent snorkeling and some of the best scuba diving in the Caribbean. If God held a painter's palette, his brush strokes, just as he brought light to the world, would paint the perfect color blue on the islands of Los Roques. Los Roques boasts one of the richest marine habitats in the Caribbean, a diver's paradise.

On a pristine sunny February day we sailed to the islands. Once the yacht anchored I went scuba diving with Camillo. Within only a brief time I saw a shark watching me from just six feet away. It was a medium-size white shark but big enough to bring terror to my mind. I was defenseless, no harpoon, no knife; my heart was going a million miles a minute. Camillo was nowhere in sight, and my breath grew short. I decided not to move and to let the currents float me away gently. Suddenly, I was pushed against a wall of coral, scratching my right side and making me bleed slightly at the hip. I knew that a shark smelling blood would attack. I had to push away from the razor-sharp coral; otherwise, I would have bled more profusely. Miraculously, after a few minutes, the shark drifted away from me. With great relief I said to myself, "Well, apparently, he does not like Italian food." The scars from the sharp coral remain to this day. When I shower and I see them, I am reminded of that moment in my life. I vowed then never to go scuba diving again, and to this day I never have.

During my daily walk around the hotel's premises one morning, I met Gary Mason from Santa Monica, California. At some point in our conversation I asked him the purpose of his visit and he said that he was going to bring a live rodeo to El Poliedro, the local sports arena. He was an impresario and booked shows around the world. I invited him for lunch at the pool's restaurant.

Nino with Sérgio Mendes, Caracas, 1979. Nino Pernetti collection.

As a result of that lunch meeting, Gary provided Las Vegas talent once a month for the hotel's ballroom. Two shows a night, seating eight hundred for dinner for the first seating and a cover charge for the second seating with beverages only. Big names performed: Dionne Warwick, Ray Conniff, Burt Bacharach, Sérgio Mendes, Donna Summer, David Soul, Diana Ross, Roberta Flack, Barry White, Gladys Knight, and Roger Williams. Gary became one of my best friends, a friendship that lasts to this day.

I have terrific memories of those years in Caracas. When the Jackson family arrived to perform at the Tamanaco, like any of the other artists, they were brought into my office to meet me and discuss their needs and performance. Michael was fifteen years old and very shy. I asked him whether he knew how to speak Spanish. He nodded and mumbled that he was from Indiana. I knew Indiana because of the Indianapolis 500. While Michael was standing there I asked him how long it took him to learn the floor staccato, going backward and jumping high in the air and landing in a split. With a big smile he said it all came natural to him. He asked his father, Joe, whether he could show me right there in my office. Michael Jackson jumped up and did a split. Who would have thought that he would become so famous? I now regret not having taken a photo at that moment.

One day in 1975 the general manager, Mr. Duwelz,

walked into my office and told me to accompany him to the Ministry of Petroleum and Natural Resources. I instructed my secretary to cancel all my morning appointments and we drove to the ministry. We entered the minister's office, and after handshakes the minister said that he intended to host the next OPEC meeting in Caracas and wanted the Tamanaco Hotel to be the venue. After all, former Venezuelan president Rómulo Betancourt had played a leading role in the creation of OPEC in 1960. Both Mr. Duwelz and I looked at each other speechless. The minister said this would be the first time that OPEC would meet outside its Vienna headquarters. Venezuela would be on every TV screen in the world, and he wanted to show the best side of the country. The minister wanted the four upper floors for the OPEC ministers, delegates, media, etc., for one week prior to and the week of the meetings. There were to be no shows during the weeklong meetings.

The meeting took place as scheduled. The whole week was like a circus or a science fiction movie. Cameramen were running up and down, television crews and sets were everywhere. Delegations spoke languages that I never knew existed, Arab representatives were all over the place with their customary kaffiyeh and robes. Everybody whispered in everyone's ears, and helicopters were flying over the hotel twenty-four hours a day. Outside there was a parade of black Rolls-Royces with drivers from India, most with Arabian royal tags. Only

Nino with the president of Venezuela, Carlos Andrés Pérez, 1977. Nino Pernetti collection.

Nino with the Swiss Gastronomy Festival, Tamanaco Hotel, Caracas, 1979. Nino Pernetti collection.

the general manager and I had security passes. Sometimes I thought the speakers were going to break into a fight, the way they were shouting in the microphone. There were people all over the place with telexes. You could hear the tapping of those small, now ancient, Olivetti typewriters in every corner. The meeting ended successfully, and the cost per barrel of oil went up.

Next, I introduced gastronomy festivals from around the world at the hotel's Le Gourmet restaurant. I would visit the country whose food we were showcasing to coordinate and meet the people, plan the menu, and import ingredients that were not available in Venezuela. The embassy of the country, in conjunction with its ministry of tourism, would provide a folkloric show to perform in the restaurant. I would provide a couple of cooks and have plenty of decorations from the country. A vendor would sell handicrafts and souvenirs at the entrance of the restaurant. This was a very popular monthlong event. Participating countries included Egypt, Indonesia, Greece, Italy, Austria, Switzerland, Thailand, Turkey, and Austria, and the state of Hawaii.

The festival's main sponsor was either the country's airline or Venezuela's Viasa airline. Sometimes the president of Venezuela would attend on opening night depending on how good relations were with the ambassador of the country in question. The gastronomy festivals were widely televised from the Tamanaco Hotel. We received great exposure and the media referred to me as the Leonardo da Vinci of the Tamanaco.,

The hotel also had a nightclub called La Boite, with a seating capacity of 150 and featuring smaller shows like Armando Manzanero, Álvarez Guedes, Nicola Di Bari, Marco Antonio Muniz, Roberto Carlos, and so on. It was open from 10:00 p.m. until breakfast.

After two years in Caracas, the home office in New York promoted me to divisional director of food and beverage operations for all four hotels in Venezuela. But the highlight of my life was not the experience of Kabul, or the Zambezi River in Africa, or the shark at Los Roques, it was when I met the legendary soccer player Pelé. Like most Italians, I am a fanatic soccer fan. During my adolescence in Italy, I spent all my leisure time watching and playing soccer. I first saw Pelé play for Brazil against Sweden on television in the 1957 World Cup championship game in Malmö, Sweden. I was twelve years old and he was only seventeen, and I remember that exceptional day as if it were yesterday. To this day nobody has matched his talent and the number of goals he scored. A person to be admired on and off the field, his voice carried the same modest warmth and enthusiasm as his personality. Pelé is my and any soccer fan's idol. In 1978 he stayed at the hotel for a two-day visit, and I quickly arranged a cocktail party for him, inviting the press, television, radio, and who's who in the world of soccer in Caracas. Then we had dinner together. The mere thought of sitting face to face with the greatest soccer player of all time put me on cloud nine.

One clear day toward the end of April, 1979, I left Caracas to explore the state of Amazonas, Venezuela, with some friends. We flew from Caracas to Puerto Ayacucho in a small plane. We rented a Jeep to go to Samariapo and from there via river transportation to

San Carlos on the border with Brazil. It was an all-day journey. The boat glided slowly through the calm waters of the river as the sky to the east was dressed in dawn tints of pink and mauve. The sound of drawn-out, guttural howls, squawks, screeches, along with the whoops and throaty cries of the forest, pulled me from my fuzzy tiredness. Within an hour I had found the howler monkey hangout and spotted toucans and herons. There were parakeets looking to feed on the ruffle palm. Hundreds of birds, some red, and some crimson orange, tawny, purple, and green, were singing a thousand tunes on every tree.

Otters barked from riverbanks, and the speckled caiman stayed on the riverbank. These leathery-skinned monsters lay immobile by the water's edge, their teeth glinting, or they glided along the river like prehistoric submarines.

I remembered these creatures from when I was in Africa. But I was disappointed not to spot any anacondas. We arrived near the village of San Carlos de Río Negro and went horseback riding on trails that led back down the hill. But the best was still to come. At a different station we rented mules to explore the rain forests. The experience became more enriching as we

Nino with legendary soccer player Pelé, Caracas, 1977. Nino Pernetti collection.

Nino and Nicola Di Bari, Caracas, 1976. Nino Pernetti collection.

learned about medicinal plants or the interrelationships of living things as well as the traditional beliefs, dialects, and society of the local Indians. We were shown the carnivorous pitcher plant. The guide told us that for 100 Bolívars (approximately $25) he could catch and throw a small monkey to the plant, but we declined the offer. We saw monkeys of all colors and sizes. Tigers hid from our inquisitive eyes. The scenery would have left most botanists and geologist speechless.

We arrived at the village (if you want to call it that) in the depths of the forest, the villagers living virtually unchanged for a millennium, in straw huts whose basic ingenuity and aesthetic beauty was striking. Exhausted, we ended the day in hammock-slung shelters deep in the forest. Strong streaks of sunlight filtered through the leaves of tall trees, the vegetation overwhelmed, while chorister robins sang in the distance.

A quick breakfast and we were back on the mules heading toward the Orinoco Basin. We were almost attacked by fiery wild peacocks, but our fearless guide knew how to disperse them. Here is where I had a memorable experience. Our guide spotted some natives in the process of herding cattle across a canal. Since it was the end of April and the dry season was ending, they had to cross the canal before the rainy season began. The canals and the Orinoco River were infested with piranhas. The guide told us to stay put and that we were going to experience a once-in-a-lifetime event. While one man loaded a small cow on the boat, another man moved the herd 100 yards farther south. When the man on the boat reached the center of the canal he took a large machete from under his belt and with a furious and skillful move he slashed the young cow's throat and quickly pushed it overboard. We looked on in frightened amazement. In seconds we saw hundreds of piranhas attack and devour the poor animal with alarming ferocity while the other cows crossed the canal safely.

After four years in Venezuela I was drafted back to the waffle-scented streets of Brussels. My former boss wanted me back. I was a bit reluctant to accept the new offer—the weather there was too rainy for me—but he told me, "Nino, do good here and we will send you to

Paris." Paris was my motivation and I decided to go back.

On the Alitalia flight to Milan from Caracas, I picked up the airline magazine. An ad about Bunratty Castle in Bunratty, five miles from Shannon Town, Ireland, caught my attention. They were using the medieval castle for special events and for tourist groups. They staged medieval-style dinners with period entertainment, décor, and food. I thought that was a good idea.

When I arrived in Brussels I was greeted by staff members I knew and by new ones. I started immediately to make phone calls to Ireland, and in a few days I was on my way to Shannon Town to contract for a package deal for a year which included artists, stage production, singers, minstrels, cooks, decorators, uniforms, and waiters. The hotel restaurant was converted into a medieval attraction. Many tourist groups came to see this spectacle, and it fascinated the locals, too.

We changed the concept of the top-floor apartments into a mini casino. In Belgium only roulette was legal, so next to the roulette tables we had a dozen dining tables, with everything cooked at tableside. Very posh and elegant!

After twelve months, I was transferred to Paris with a promotion to executive assistant manager at the Paris Sheraton Hotel, a 1,000-room hotel with four restaurants and banquet facilities for 1,500 people. It was the biggest and tallest hotel in Paris. Everyone should live in Paris at least once in this lifetime. They should spend springtime and summer in Paris so they can sample heaven.

For the two days before going to Paris I could not sleep. The ultimate goal, dream, and ambition of a hotelman was to be placed in Paris. This was the culmination of a career. It was like reaching the peak of Mount Everest. Paris was the capital of gastronomy, with the very best in food, wines, and hotels in the world, and where eating well was not an option, it was a duty. I had prepared and waited for this day. Now a dream was coming true after all those years of training, learning, traveling, and adventures. This was France, where good cooking was regarded as a combination of national sport and high art, and wine was always served with lunch and dinner.

At first I was a bit intimidated by Paris. It stimulated the senses, demanding to be seen, heard, touched, tasted, and smelled. From romance in the beautiful parks, to landscapes on bus-sized canvases, to small cafés with people discussing the uses of garlic or the finer points of comedian Jerry Lewis, Paris was the essence of all things French. To experience Paris one must gaze rapturously at its breezy boulevards, impressive monuments, great works of art and magical lights, savor its cheeses, pastries, wines, and seafood, feel the wind in one's face while strolling along the River Seine or a frisson of fear and pleasure atop the Eiffel Tower. I would say that of all the cities I have lived in I favor Paris above all.

However, winters were cold and harsh. Most of the population stayed indoors, at home by the fire, eating roasted chestnuts. The streets and sidewalk cafés were full on the inside but empty on the outside, and the city was gray.

FERDIE: How did you manage in Paris?

NINO: Since I was to be at the Paris Sheraton, I was exposed to the finest cooking and many extraordinary ways to prepare and serve food. They knew gastronomy, but I knew command. I knew I was the boss and so I took over. Soon after I arrived, I assembled the staff. I sat at the head of the table and, looking everyone directly in the eye before speaking in my best French, I said, "I'm the general." I wanted to sound like Napoleon because, after all, Napoleon was born when Corsica was still Italian territory and his real name was Napoleone Buonaparte. "You're my troops. I need soldiers around me who will follow my orders!" I wanted to make a statement right from the beginning that I was there to succeed with their help.

FERDIE: Under your guidance the Paris Sheraton became one of the best American hotels in Paris. Tell us how you did it.

NINO: The difference, I knew, was that under American management you must show a profit, upward movement. It's not about maintaining centuries-old traditions, it's about going to the bank. After being there for one month I started to revolutionize the food and beverage departments. I hired Raoul Gaiga, winner of the Meilleurs Ouvriers de France [France's highest cooking award] and twice of the Amis d'Escoffier medal, as executive chef. He was very talented, one of the best chefs in Paris. An immediate chemistry developed between us, and we are still in touch.

Raoul was instrumental in guiding me through the French gastronomical tradition and idiosyncrasies. He took me under his wing and together we prepared menus we both knew well, culinary and commercially. The hotel was patronized mostly by foreigners, so the restaurants had to have menus with a different approach. Gone were the long preparations of traditional French specialties. In their place came the introduction of modern dishes, simpler, less sauce, less cream, faster preparation, larger portions. I included a few Italian specialties like pasta, fish, and veal scaloppine, too. Our motto was "Give the customers what they like." American wines had started to be introduced in the European market, so I featured some of them on the wine list, despite the big "Mon Dieu!" from the sommelier.

Nino at a special dinner with Chef Raoul Gaiga at Cave Veuve Clicquot, Epernay, 1981. Nino Pernetti collection.

Nino with the Sheraton Hotel staff, Paris, 1982. Nino Pernetti collection.

We had to develop our own identity and marketing plan. The first few months at each executive meeting I always talked enthusiastically. I made most of the department heads raise their eyebrows but, in the end, revenues increased substantially. I knew we could not compete with many of the other fine restaurants in Paris, but with a great chef like Raoul Gaiga at my side and by converting to modern cooking, we made headlines in the local newspapers and popular Parisian magazines.

To get to know Paris I took advantage of my senior assistant, François Velay. He was an avid jogger and, being an athlete myself, we ran together once a week through Paris, seeing the sights along the way. We selected special routes, through the Bois de Boulogne or the Jardins de Luxembourg; there is no better way to familiarize yourself with a city than by running through it. We would pass the imposing neoclassical Arc de Triomphe and go down one of the twelve avenues leading to, unquestionably, the world's largest traffic roundabout. We would circle Notre Dame Cathedral two or three times to admire its architecture, a marvel

Nino running a marathon in Paris
with his assistant, François Velay,
1982. Nino Pernetti collection.

of medieval engineering, and to look at the cathedral's
frightening gargoyles. We soon formed a small team of
runners, and once a month we raced to Versailles, fifteen miles one way, and returned by train. We had lunch
around the Château de Versailles. We stipulated that the
last to arrive would pick up 50 percent of the tab. I never
arrived last so many times in my life in any sporting
event like the run from Paris to Versailles. The manage-
rial reward for finishing the race last was that I was able
to create a great spirit of camaraderie with the staff.

The hotel was the place to stay for international fi-
nanciers, fashion and media executives, and other well-
heeled travelers. It was the grand dame, its lobby and
fashionable bars, popular meeting places. Also well liked
was the newly created pastry shop, where hotel guests
indulged in creative petits fours and Parisians bought
gorgeous cakes and pastries. The rooms, though rather
small, were sleek and modern and had a spectacular
panoramic view of the city.

FERDIE: Ever adaptable to the ways of the business community, you experienced some unforeseen challenges on the road. One day the sommelier, Monsieur Jobin, came to your office and asked you if you would like to accompany him to a rare-vintage wine tasting in the city. Tell us what happened next.

Nino leaning on a statue of Dom Perignon, Epernay, 1981. Nino Pernetti collection.

Nino learning about champagne at Cave Veuve Clicquot, Epernay, 1981. Nino Pernetti collection.

NINO: Well, the story is really about how much this trade had evolved and changed. Protocol today is definitely different. I remember it was almost noon and I had not eaten. Because for our own wine tastings we provided food, I assumed that there would be hors d'oeuvres. I noticed that many of the French experts brought their own brown bags. Now I was stuck sipping glass after glass of dozens of bottles of red and white wines. This was not a good thing, for by the end of the tasting I was just not very comfortable. Mr. Jobin was having even greater difficulties with hand-eye coordination. When the manager of the wine tasting handed us a $450 bill, I thought he had had too much to drink as well. Mr. Jobin felt embarrassed for not having told me that you paid for a wine tasting when rare vintage wines were sampled. He confessed to me that he had not anticipated such a high amount and that he had not brought any money. I realized that I had left my wallet in the office.

The manager in charge of the tasting went stone-faced, saying that we had to pay before he would allow us to leave. No credit cards, no checks, just $450 in cash. This irritated me tremendously, for here I was, a manager at the Paris Sheraton Hotel, and I could not believe that we would not be trusted to drive to the hotel to get the money. I called the hotel's chief accountant, who drove over with the cash. I had learned yet another lesson for my around-the-world cookbook.

FERDIE: One of your most memorable moments in Paris occurred when you were having dinner with a wine supplier at the hotel's Montparnasse Restaurant. Marcello Mastroianni, Catherine Deneuve, and their young daughter, Chiara, walked in to have dinner. They sat down at a nice window table and ordered a 1962 Romanée Conti, one of the great wines of Burgundy. Nino, tell us that story.

NINO: I jumped up from my table and went to greet them. You can imagine my excitement meeting them in person. These were legends of the movie world. I was nervous and incoherent. Mr. Mastroianni asked me if he could have a simple plate of linguini with garlic and olive oil and penne carbonara for Catherine and Chiara. Full of emotion I said, "Con molto piacere, Signor Mastroianni" [With great pleasure, Mr. Mastroianni], not remembering that I had no Italian cooks working at the hotel. So I went into the kitchen and put on an apron and began to prepare the pasta. I had not held a cooking pan since my days at the hotel school. But I never forgot what I learned. When Mastroianni finished his meal, he wanted to meet and thank the chef who had prepared the pasta. So I called for Chef Gaiga to come out and answer any questions. I was there just in case I was needed, but Signor Mastroianni commended him for the delicious pasta and obliged us with a photo together, which I kept for years but lost when I moved to North America.

FERDIE: The "Nino touch" brought in an important customer. The mayor of Paris in 1981 was Jacques Chirac. Occasionally, Mr. Chirac came to the Sheraton to have lunch. You noticed that he loved to end his meal with a good cheese.

NINO: Oh, how that man loved cheese. I summoned to my office the maître d,' Monsieur Pollard, and instructed him to prepare a cheese display cart of fifty to sixty of the best and rarest cheeses as a permanent feature. At his next visit the cart was wheeled to Mr. Chirac, compliments of the house. From that day on Mayor Chirac ate at the Paris Sheraton regularly. He was very sorry to see me leave. Of course, Jacques Chirac eventually became the president of France. My other motto was "No request is forgotten, no detail left unattended."

The general manager, Canada-born Jules Prevost, told me that he was going to resign to take over Holiday Inn International as president and wanted to know if I was interested in joining him as the vice president of food and beverage for the Caribbean, Mexico, and South America Division. I would have an office in Miami, Florida, and I would report to the home office in Memphis, Tennessee. We stared at each other for a few seconds. I was pleased at the idea of going to the beautiful city of Miami, having visited a few times when I was working in Caracas. The offer interested me, and he made it more appealing when he told me that I would be in charge of fifteen hotels, in Freeport, Nassau, Aruba, Montego Bay, Acapulco, Central America, and South America down to São Paulo, Brazil. My adrenaline was pumping and I was torn between the glamour of Paris and the tropical sun of the south. I asked him if I could visit the hotels before accepting the offer.

I opted for Miami. For that job I traveled to Nassau and Freeport, then through Central America to San José, Costa Rica. From there I went to Tegucigalpa, Honduras, and to Montego Bay, Jamaica. In the world's highest city in Bolivia, it was hard for me to breathe because of the thin air. After going to Mexico City I went to the vibrant city of São Paulo, where many Italian immigrants came to work the coffee plantations in the 1800s. Then I went on to Rio de Janeiro, Santos, Brasília, and back to Caracas and the Bahamas. It was twenty-one days of travel each month, then home for barely a week. After four years I began to explore the possibility of working outside of the hotel chains.

SIDE DISHES

Artichokes Roman Style

Carciofi alla Romana

6 medium globe artichokes

½ cup extra-virgin olive oil

6 garlic cloves, minced

4 fresh mint sprigs, leaves only

½ cup dry white wine

1 lemon

1 tablespoon minced fresh Italian parsley, leaves only

Salt and pepper

Trim the leaves of the artichokes down to the yellow heart. Peel the stems and cut off the greenish tops down to the heart and leave a one-inch stem.

Heat the olive oil in a large skillet with a lid over medium heat until hot but not smoking. Add the artichokes. Cook for a few minutes until golden, turning once, and then add the garlic and mint and season with salt and pepper to taste. Cover and simmer 6–8 minutes, then add the wine, lower the heat, cover, and continue cooking 15–20 minutes, until the artichokes are tender.

Squeeze lemon juice and sprinkle parsley over each artichoke. Serves 6.

Braised Fennel

Finocchi Brasati

6 tablespoons extra-virgin olive oil, divided

3 fresh fennel bulbs, each cut lengthwise into 6 wedges

⅓ cup minced onion

½ teaspoon grated fresh lemon peel

1½ tablespoons fresh lemon juice

1½ tablespoons minced fresh Italian parsley

1 garlic clove, minced

Salt and pepper

Preheat the oven to 400°F.

Heat 2 tablespoons olive oil in a large skillet over high heat until hot but not smoking. Add half the fennel and sauté until deep golden brown on all sides, about 10 minutes. Transfer the fennel to a ceramic or glass baking dish. Repeat with the remaining fennel.

Mix the onion, lemon peel, lemon juice, parsley, and garlic in a medium bowl. Whisk in 2 tablespoons olive oil and drizzle the mixture over the fennel. Cover the dish with foil and bake 25 minutes. Remove the foil and bake until the fennel is tender and the onions begin to brown, 20 minutes longer. Serves 6.

Cauliflower Milanese

Cavolfiori alla Milanese

1 tablespoon coarse salt

1 whole cauliflower

2 eggs, slightly beaten

1 cup fresh plain bread crumbs
(from a baguette)

1 tablespoon unsalted butter

Salt and pepper

Bring a pot of water to a boil. Add the coarse salt and the cauliflower and cook for 8 minutes. Remove the cauliflower, drain, and cool. When it is cool, cut it into ¼-inch thick slices. Lightly salt the beaten eggs. Dip the cauliflower slices in the eggs, then in the bread crumbs, patting softly to help the crumbs adhere.

Melt the butter in a nonstick pan over high heat. When the butter begins foaming, add the cauliflower slices in a single layer. Lower the heat to medium-low and cook 7–8 minutes, turning frequently, until golden. Season with salt and pepper to taste. Serves 6.

Eggplant with Tomatoes

Melanzane con Pomodori

1 medium (1½ pounds) eggplant, diced

½ cup coarse salt

⅓ cup extra-virgin olive oil

1 garlic clove, crushed

3 medium plum tomatoes, diced

1 tablespoon minced fresh Italian parsley, plus extra for garnish

1 teaspoon cracked black pepper

Salt

Wash the eggplant, leaving the skin on, and cut into cubes. Toss the cubes with the coarse salt to coat and drain for 1 hour in a colander. The salt will draw the excess liquid from the eggplant.

Gently squeeze the eggplant to remove excess moisture and pat dry with paper towels. Heat the olive oil in a large, heavy skillet over medium heat until hot but not smoking. Add the garlic, sauté for 1 minute, and remove it. Add the eggplant and cook for 5 minutes, stirring frequently. Stir in the tomatoes and parsley and continue cooking over medium heat, stirring frequently, 15–20 minutes. Add the pepper and cook for an additional minute. Season with salt to taste and garnish with parsley. Serves 6.

Garlic Mashed Potatoes

Purè di Patate con Aglio

2½ pounds red potatoes, unpeeled, cubed

4 garlic cloves, peeled and thinly sliced

1 cup low-fat milk

4 tablespoons unsalted butter

1 teaspoon ground nutmeg

¾ teaspoon salt

¼ teaspoon cracked black pepper

Place the potatoes and garlic in a large saucepan, cover with cold water, and bring to a boil over high heat. Reduce the heat and simmer, uncovered, until the potatoes are tender when pierced with a knife, about 20 minutes. Drain the potatoes and return to the pot over low heat. Discard the garlic.

Add the milk, butter, nutmeg, salt, and pepper. Mash with a potato masher to the desired consistency. Serves 6.

Oven-fried Potatoes

Patatine al Forno

3 pounds baking potatoes, scrubbed, peeled, cut into ⅓-inch wide fries

½ cup extra-virgin olive oil

1 tablespoon minced Italian parsley

Salt

Preheat the oven to 450°F.

Soak the potatoes for 20 minutes in a large bowl of cold water. Drain them well and pat dry with paper towels.

In a large bowl, toss the potatoes with the olive oil and sprinkle with salt to taste.

Spread the potatoes on a large nonstick rimmed baking sheet in a single layer. Bake for 25 minutes. Turn and bake for an additional 25 minutes, turning occasionally, until golden and crisp. Sprinkle with parsley before serving. Serves 6.

Oven-roasted Tomatoes

Pomodori al Forno

12 plum tomatoes, halved lengthwise and seeded

3 tablespoons extra-virgin olive oil

8 large garlic cloves, minced

2 tablespoons minced fresh thyme

1 tablespoon dried oregano

Salt and pepper

Preheat the oven to 250°F.

Toss the tomato halves with the olive oil, garlic, thyme, and oregano and season with salt and pepper to taste. Arrange the tomatoes, cut side down, on a rack set on a rimmed baking sheet and roast for 2½ hours. Remove the tomatoes from the oven and peel, discarding the skins. Return the tomatoes to the oven and roast until they are dry but still pliable, about 1½ hours. Cool to room temperature. Serves 6.

Parmesan and Chive Potato Gratin

Patate Gratinate al Parmigiano

2½ pounds red potatoes
unpeeled, cubed

4 garlic cloves, thinly sliced

1 cup whole milk

2½ tablespoons unsalted
butter

¾ cup freshly grated
Parmesan cheese

¼ cup fresh bread crumbs
(from a baguette)

¼ cup minced fresh chives

Salt and pepper

Preheat the broiler on high.

Place the potatoes and garlic in a large saucepan, cover with cold water, and bring to a boil over high heat. Reduce the heat and simmer, uncovered, until the potatoes are tender when pierced with a knife, about 20 minutes. Drain and discard the garlic. Return the potatoes to the pot over low heat.

Stir in the milk and butter and season with salt and pepper to taste. Mash the potatoes with a potato masher to the desired consistency.

Transfer the potatoes to a shallow 1½-quart ovenproof casserole or baking dish. Combine the cheese, bread crumbs, and chives and sprinkle evenly over the potatoes. Broil 4–5 inches from the heat, until the cheese melts and starts to brown, 3–4 minutes. Serves 6.

Polenta

3 cups water

1 teaspoon salt

2 cups whole milk

1½ cups coarse yellow cornmeal

1 tablespoon freshly grated Parmesan cheese

Pour the water into a large, heavy saucepan. Add the salt and bring to a boil. Heat the milk in a separate pan while the water is coming to a boil.

Reduce the heat so the water is barely simmering. Hold half of the cornmeal in your hand and let it pour through your fingers in a very slow, steady stream, stirring constantly in the same direction with a wooden spoon to prevent it from clumping. Add one cup of milk, continuing to stir. Add the rest of the cornmeal in the same manner and add the rest of the milk. Add the Parmesan and continue stirring for about 40 minutes.

Divide the polenta evenly among 4 plates. With the back of the wooden spoon, pat it down to form a mini pizza. Serves 4.

Sautéed Mushrooms and Baby Onions

Funghi e Cipolline Saltati

1½ cups peeled baby onions

2 tablespoons extra-virgin olive oil

1 teaspoon unsalted butter

1½ cups mixed mushrooms, sliced

1½ cups béchamel sauce (see recipe, page 59)

½ cup minced Italian parsley

Salt and pepper

Bring a pan of salted water to a boil and boil the onions for 5 minutes. Drain them well. Heat the olive oil and butter until hot but not smoking. Sauté the mushrooms 2 minutes. Add the onions and cook for 3 minutes, stirring constantly. Season with salt and pepper to taste. Stir in the béchamel sauce and parsley and cook for 2 minutes, stirring occasionally. Serves 6.

Spinach Purée

Purè di Spinaci

2 pounds fresh spinach

½ cup heavy cream

4 tablespoons unsalted butter

½ teaspoon ground nutmeg

2½ tablespoons freshly grated Parmesan cheese

Salt and pepper

Place the spinach in a sink full of room-temperature water; stir to remove dirt. Remove the spinach from the sink, add fresh water, and repeat as many times as needed to remove all dirt. Drain the spinach in a colander.

Bring a stockpot of cold water to a boil on medium-high heat. Add the spinach and cook 4–5 minutes. Remove the spinach while it is still green and place it in cold water to stop the cooking. Drain it well and squeeze it with your hands to remove excess water. Place the spinach in a blender and purée.

Pour the cream into a medium skillet and cook over medium-high heat until it is reduced by half. Place the spinach purée in another medium skillet over low-medium heat. Add the butter and nutmeg and stir until the butter melts. Add the Parmesan and cream to the spinach and bring to a boil, stirring constantly. Season with salt and pepper to taste. Serves 6.

Stuffed Tomatoes

Pomodori Ripieni Gratinati

6 medium tomatoes

3 tablespoons extra-virgin olive oil

1 oil-packed anchovy, minced

1 tablespoon minced onion

1 garlic clove, smashed

2 cups fresh plain bread crumbs (use a baguette)

2 tablespoons minced fresh Italian parsley

1 teaspoon minced fresh oregano

¼ cup freshly grated Parmesan cheese

Salt and pepper

Preheat the oven to 350°F. Oil an oven-proof baking pan and set aside.

Cut a thin slice from the stem end of each tomato and, with your fingers, remove the seeds and the pulp without breaking the skin. Place the tomato shells in the baking pan. Combine the olive oil, anchovy, onion, and garlic in a sauté pan and cook at medium-low for 4–5 minutes, until the onion turns a light golden color. Remove the pan from the heat.

Combine the bread crumbs, parsley, oregano, and salt and pepper to taste in a bowl. Add the mixture to the onion mixture and combine well. Fill the tomato shells with the mixture. Bake 20 minutes. Sprinkle each tomato with Parmesan and bake for an additional 2 minutes. Serves 6.

Stuffed Zucchini

Zucchini Ripieni

6 6-ounce zucchini

3 tablespoons extra-virgin olive oil

½ cup minced onion

½ cup minced celery

½ cup minced carrots

3 garlic cloves, minced

3 bay leaves

2 tablespoons fresh rosemary

3 tablespoon dry white wine

1 pound ground pork

½ cup fresh bread crumbs (use a baguette)

½ cup freshly grated Parmesan cheese

3 tablespoons unsalted butter, divided

Salt and pepper

Preheat the oven to 375°F.

Cut the zucchini in half lengthwise. Using a small spoon, scoop out the flesh and discard it. Season the zucchini shells with salt and pepper to taste and drain upside down for 15 minutes.

Heat the olive oil in a heavy skillet until hot but not smoking. Add the onion, celery, carrots, garlic, and bay leaves and cook over low heat until the vegetables are soft but not brown, about 8 minutes. Remove the pan from the heat, discard the bay leaves, and add the rosemary and wine. Stir in the ground pork, season with salt and pepper to taste, and cook over moderately low heat, breaking up the meat, until it is mostly white. Remove the pan from the heat and stir in the bread crumbs and Parmesan.

Divide the stuffing evenly among the zucchini and dot with butter. Place the stuffed zucchini in a baking dish and add water to a depth of ½ inch. Cover the pan with foil and bake for 15 minutes. Serve 6.

Nino at Caffè Baci, Miami, 1986. Photo by Allen Malschick.

NINE

Miami

Nino Establishes His Own Restaurant

FERDIE: You wanted the perfect Italian restaurant, but two attempts did not meet your high standards, so how did you rethink the problem at the time?

NINO: I came very close to throwing in the towel. I contemplated the possibility of working once again for a hotel chain. Then, in a conversation with my friend Giorgio Bibolini, an architect and interior designer of great taste, we concocted the idea of opening a restaurant. He brought the financial backing needed to open such a restaurant and we became partners. Thus Caffè Baci was born.

I loved Miami—the way of life, the cosmopolitan city throbbing with excitement, money, power, elegance, jet-setters, politics, intrigue, and a media explosion—that was the formula for success! Location, location!

Coral Gables at that time was a laid-back yet elegant, family-oriented affluent city. At 2522 Ponce De Leon Boulevard there was a French bistro called Angela's Café. My intuition told me that this was a great spot to launch my restaurant.

On an unusually hot day in mid-January 1985, shortly before lunch, I walked into Angela's Café and sat down at one of the tables near the entrance. Before asking what I would like, the owner ran toward me and said, "No lunch before noon." No wonder I was the only patron. I introduced myself and within one week we closed the deal.

FERDIE: Caffè Baci was small and cozy, seating fifty-five, with pleasing pinkish fabric on the walls and a high arched bronzed ceiling. It was unique, different from anything you could find in Coral Gables or Miami at that time. This was the end of the line that started with that energetic thirteen-year-old boy preparing espressos in Limone, Italy. You put to use all that you had learned, but one thing that had never changed was your desire to make customers feel comfortable and properly attended.

NINO: We went in with a rather elegant and simple idea: Let me show you how to prepare and enjoy Italian food that is not fattening. Still, in those days, many Italian restaurants were associated with red-checkered tablecloths, Chianti bottles, and spaghetti with meatballs. All for $12.50.

Tony Bennett at Caffè Abbracci, Miami, 1995. Nino Pernetti collection.

FERDIE: Nino, you fit into the niche between cheap food and quality-priced food. You had your own new menu and offered moderate prices in a luxurious locale. From the opening weeks, Gableites said, "Let's go to Nino's," never "Let's go to Baci's. Caffè Baci began to make noise. It appeared in *Travel and Leisure*, *USA Today*, *Esquire*, and *Gourmet*.

NINO: Celebrities succumbed to its lure. Here is one of those many moments. Late on a Sunday, Andy Rooney came running into the restaurant for a quick meal. I was just closing. "Sorry, we're closed," I said.

"Can't you keep it open for me?" responded Rooney.

"Sorry, I was just waiting for a TV program to finish so I could go home."

"What were you watching?" said Rooney.

"*60 Minutes*, of course. I never miss it." I smiled and Rooney laughed at my response. Of course, he did not go away hungry.

FERDIE: It soon became evident that Caffè Baci was not large enough to accommodate the demand. The harder you worked, the more people came, and the less you could accommodate them and give them the service you liked to provide.

NINO: Caffè Baci was busy from day one. People were not too happy having to wait while standing. Furthermore, Caffè Baci did not have a liquor license, so only wine and beer could be served. In those days small seating capacity meant you could not obtain a liquor license, nor could you buy one.

In early December 1988, Villa d'Este Restaurant in Coral Gables was going to close. It was the opportunity I had been waiting for. It and the space next door would give me the 4,000 square feet I needed to qualify for a liquor license.

I wanted to make a small bar that would be not only an asset but also an attraction. Thus the natural name progression: *Baci* (Hugs) to *Abbracci* (Kisses). My partner, Giorgio Bibolini, immediately went to the drawing board.

Now I had my work cut out for me, because I had leased not only an existing restaurant but also the space next door, which used to be a beauty salon. Giorgio and his team of designers had a lot of work to do but the outcome was an exquisite design for the new restaurant. I loved the arched ceiling at Caffè Baci's and I wanted the same barrel vault with the same effect at Caffè Abbracci. The bar was nice and comfortable. It was my stolen bread. It was a place to socialize and enjoy a drink before dinner.

My concept of the restaurant was a home with three rooms. Caffè Abbracci was designed to vary from room

Nino with Elie Wiesel, Caffè Abbracci, Miami, 1999. Nino Pernetti collection.

to room, as a house would, but to share the same design theme, with all the materials understated but expensive looking. Dark green marble repeats from room to room. The bar is a sleek space of different wood, marble, and mirrors. This was the first restaurant with a bar in Coral Gables. The restrooms had to be the best in town; this was very important.

Italian restaurants continue to be among the most popular and most competitive. So I hired as executive chef Mauro Bazzanini, a native of Bologna, Italy, the pasta-making capital. Mauro, a young chef, was very talented and intuitive. He understood perfectly that what was needed was food that other Italian restaurants weren't serving, with no gimmickry attached to it, and he executed it. Carpaccio was a must. Basically, it was the same kind of food as at Caffè Baci—everything fresh.

Nino tasting bread at the National Restaurant Association Show in Chicago, 1984. Nino Pernetti collection.

FERDIE: What else did you need to make it work?

NINO: I gathered samples of tablecloths, flatware, and glasses and I set tables with different tablecloths, dishes, and silver patterns. Tablecloths were chosen, washed, bleached, and ironed. Dishes full of baked-on sauce were run through the dishwasher, all to see how they stood up and how they looked.

The china had to be ordered. At first I chose a white bone china with a subtle embossed rim but changed my mind because the sauces didn't look good with the indentation. I chose plain Dudson off-white china because food looked good on it.

If you don't have the right players, you are not a winning team. I hired a competent manager, Paolo Retani, with a lot of experience and well known to the community. He would know who was who as they entered the restaurant. Chef Mauro spent weeks perfecting the menu.

I interviewed candidates for the kitchen and waiters for the dining room but left the final decisions to the chef and the manager. Staff consisted of fifteen cooks and six dishwashers. Thirty waiters and busboys were assigned for the opening along with four cashiers, two bookkeepers, and four bartenders.

New chairs—no money spared here as they had to be comfortable, with high backs and rich upholstery. How many round, square, and extra-large tables should be ordered? Table selection was very important. A new and wider awning was a must for when it rained. The goal was to have a restaurant that looked like a million dollars but that cost only half that, because Giorgio was going to use the restaurant as a showcase.

Another important issue when opening a restaurant is your credit and standing with banks. It's easier to open a restaurant when you have already been in business for some time, because you have an established relationship with lenders and vendors. It is not cheap. It costs a lot of money, and I could have bought a nice house on the water in Coconut Grove instead.

Nino with Gabriela Sabatini, who is celebrating her win at the Key Biscayne Tournament, at Caffè Baci, 1986. Nino Pernetti collection.

Nino with flamenco dancers Clarita Filgueiras and Timo Lozano, Caffè Abbracci, Miami, 2007. Photo by Luisita Sevilla Pacheco.

Nino running in the Miami marathon with friend Ed Walton, 1984. Nino Pernetti collection.

FERDIE: How does it feel being an owner of one restaurant then opening another at the same time?

NINO: Either you have it or you don't. Being a restaurant owner isn't easy. I was like a juggler trying to balance two balls at once. The construction of Caffè Abbracci and the regular schedule of Caffè Baci kept me very busy. I worked seven days a week, sixteen hours a day trying to keep up. After almost six months, Caffè Abbracci was ready. It opened its doors to the public on June 15, 1989.

Though the restaurants were only a few blocks from each other, the distance was huge. Since Caffè Baci was already established, I initially dedicated more time to Caffè Abbracci, because it was newer and larger, and left the operation of Caffè Baci in the hands of its manager, Domenico Diana. But as time went by, I realized that I could not be in two places at the same time. When making reservations customers were constantly asking where I would be that night, at Caffè Baci or Caffè Abbracci. This created confusion and, more important, I could not control both restaurants 100 percent. After three years, I started thinking about selling Caffè Baci in order to focus only on Caffè Abbracci.

FERDIE: Nino, while you were thinking about the sale of Caffè Baci you remembered one of its magical moments. It was the week of January 22, 1989, when the Super Bowl was held in Miami. In the days leading to the game, the 49ers' great quarterback, Joe Montana, came for dinner every night with his wife, Jennifer. You would fix them a nice Italian dinner. (Montana's grandfather was Italian.) The night before the game you prepared a plate of penne with julienne of beef tenderloin marinated in a balsamic reduction then grilled and served with oven-roasted tomatoes.

NINO: And that is what I recommended to him. "Joe, this will give your arm the strength it needs to guide you to a touchdown to win the Super Bowl."

He laughed and said, "Nino what kind of prophecy is that?"

"It is not a prophecy, it is a reality," I responded with a smile.

The 49ers were trailing 13 to 16 with 34 seconds remaining. Montana, in a cold-blooded risk, threw a very long pass for a touchdown, and they won the Super Bowl 20 to 16.

The game had been over for a long time, but I was still at Caffè Baci when the phone rang. Joe Montana asked for me and said, "Nino, you were right, that pasta did give my arm the strength needed for a touchdown." I felt so good that a champion like Montana gave me a call that night. Special moments like these don't come often.

Jerry Rice and Joe Montana at Caffè Baci, Coral Gables, 1989. Nino Pernetti collection.

FERDIE: At the end of June 1992, you received word that your mother, back in Italy, was terminally ill with cancer and had three to five weeks to live. You were getting ready to go to Italy when, on a Tuesday morning two days before your departure, while you were giving instructions to Domenico at Caffè Baci's, an Italian gentleman walked in, looking for all the world like a very prosperous Milan merchant banker. He introduced himself as Carlo Rossi and asked if he could talk with you for a minute. Politely, you declined, saying you were busy getting ready for a trip to Italy and that you also had to go to Caffè Abbracci for lunch. Mr. Rossi said that he wanted to make an offer to purchase Caffè Baci. That got your attention.

NINO: "Let's have an espresso," I said. The first question I asked Rossi was why he wanted to purchase Caffè Baci. I expected the usual answer—as an investment. But he had a different story. He wanted to buy the restaurant for his daughter. Mr. Rossi looked like a gentleman and had the financial means. I listened and told him again that I had to leave for Italy in two days and suggested we resume the conversation upon my return. Then I told him about my dying mother. Mr. Rossi asked me where I was from and I told him Salò, Lago di Garda. Mr. Rossi told me that he was from Milan and that we could work out the details in Salò if I liked. I did not think that was a good idea, since that was where I would be grieving for my mother. We decided to meet in Milan, where I could stay overnight with my eldest brother, Plinio. We shook hands.

On the day of our appointment Mr. Rossi picked me up from my brother's apartment in Milan and drove me to his house, where I met his wife, Federica, and his other daughter. We had dinner at Il Contadino behind the Piazza Duomo, obviously his favorite, because he was well received and warmly greeted by the owners and staff alike. I said to myself, "This is Caffè Abbracci."

Mr. Rossi was prepared and he meant business. He opened his jacket and took out a little notebook and with a gold Mont Blanc pen took down notes and scribbled numbers. He told the maître d' no menu was needed, that he would order, if I didn't mind. I said fine, although I wanted very much to see the menu to scout interesting dishes.

While we sipped the traditional Campari soda before the first course arrived, I asked him, "Why Caffè Baci?"

With a nice smile almost hidden below his black moustache, he said, "I fell in love with it. I had been going with my real estate agent through all the Italian restaurants in Dade County and Broward, and Caffè Baci is what I liked for my daughter Federica. It has an angelic feel that no other restaurants have. It is a friendly restaurant."

The dinner was very good. We feasted on dish after dish, washed down by an exquisite 1982 Tignanello. At any minute I expected him to ask my selling price,

but he waited until dessert was served. I told him, "Mr. Rossi, what if I do not want to sell?"

He said, "You would not be here if you didn't want to sell, and may I add something? We met at the perfect time. You have your reasons to sell."

I thought he was right. While savoring a delicious mini pear tart topped with a Marsala sauce, Mr. Rossi took his glasses off and said, "Nino, how much do you want?"

I gave my price, and Mr. Rossi, without blinking an eye, said, "It is a good, fair price." After we discussed the details of the sale, he said, "I will fly back to Miami next week and I will instruct my lawyer to prepare all the necessary transfer papers so that upon your return everything will be ready."

FERDIE: The deal included your giving him two months support and introducing the customers to Federica as the new owner. The restaurant was to be handed over "as is," including the staff and the food and beverage stock.

NINO: Mr. Rossi drove me back to my brother's apartment that night. I didn't know whether I felt miserable or happy. In reality, Caffè Baci would have gone soon. Sentimentally, I did not want to let go, as I felt like I was losing my best friend.

Domenico Diana, manager of Caffè Baci, 1989. Photo by Allen Malschick.

FERDIE: Your mother died and was buried in Salò next to your father, who had passed away two years earlier. It was a heartbreaking time.

NINO: I was in Miami when my father died and now I buried them side by side. When I returned to Miami, thoughts of home were constantly on my mind. I remembered with fondness the last years of my parents' lives, when I would go home to visit them on vacation and my mom would cook while I sat in the kitchen sipping a glass of wine with Papá. Mamma would say with such joy, "Nino, I prepared the food you always liked when you were young." She always went out of her way to please me or maybe to reward me for having been the backbone of the family and for having kept everyone together.

One time she was cooking something new for me, and I asked her what it was. She answered in a cheerful voice, "It is pointless to explain the recipe to you because you would not understand it anyway."

I smiled, shrugged my shoulders, and said, "Yes, you are right, Mamma." For her I was still the little Nino who left Italy for Germany as a busboy in search of success. I still say to this day that the best food I have ever eaten came from my Mamma's kitchen.

I remember a hot summer evening when my father and I were in the garden drinking red Bardolino while Mamma was upstairs preparing dinner. I had always longed to ask him a question about our childhood: "Papá, why were you so severe and strict with all of us and not so much with Massimo?"

He said, "I know and I realized it. Massimo is her

son, and maybe I did it in tribute to your mother for having taken care of all of you with such tender love."

I looked him in the eye and, with a Mona Lisa smile, raised my glass in acknowledgment as we toasted. I understood and no more words were spoken. We drank silently, sealing this chapter of our life as father and son.

Brothers *(from left)* Bruno, Olivo, Nino, and Diego, and two-year-old Tatiana, Brescia, 1997. Nino Pernetti collection.

FERDIE: Your thoughts returned to Miami and eventually your good business sense took over; the Caffè Baci era was over. From the proceeds, you bought out your partner, Giorgio, and became the sole owner of Caffè Abbracci. A new stage started for you.

NINO: I was determined to make Caffè Abbracci an institution, a restaurant that would stand out for its décor and its northern Italian cooking. I enjoyed making customers happy, and I wanted everyone who came into Caffè Abbracci to feel like they had walked into my home.

I compare running a restaurant to a Broadway play. You enter, the curtain goes up, and the show starts. The staff must put on a great show day after day, year after year. It is like being on stage, constantly performing, and you must give your best. Every day is show time; you are the director, the staff, the actors. They must be entertaining yet polite; they must be flamboyant yet respectful; they must be informative yet diplomatic.

FERDIE: You say you have never had any gimmick or special event such as happy hour or theme event or special wine pairing dinner, because you do not want to be in fashion today and out tomorrow.

NINO: Once while in Florence I saw a majestic, colorful floral stained-glass ceiling at an antiques store. I knew it would look beautiful in Caffè Abbracci. I immediately asked the store owner if I could make a phone call to Miami. The owner, sensing a potential sale, guided me to his office. I asked my manager, Loris, to measure the bar ceiling. It turned out it would fit perfectly. I went back into the shop and, not knowing the cost, tried to hide my enthusiasm in order to bargain. But the owner, an old man with miles of experience, understood that I wanted the stained glass and did not budge on the price. The stained-glass is now in the bar at Caffè Abbracci and is admired by the customers while they sip their favorite drink.

FERDIE: In Miami, fine dining is constantly evolving and highly competitive. It takes creative thinking and precise planning to stay above the competition. How do you keep this love affair with our city going, Nino?

NINO: I am a passionate man. I take special pleasure in knowing my customers will relish the smallest detail. So the centerpieces in the middle of each dining room are always breathtaking, as are the orchids on each table and the fresh flowers in the ladies' room. Food and flowers go hand in hand. Food would conquer any mind and flowers would conquer any heart, both bringing joy and happiness.

One day not too long ago, I was sound asleep when the phone rang at about 2:30 a.m. I was in a daze. On the line was a regular customer, saying that he was locked inside the restaurant. That got my attention immediately. I turned on the lights and said, "Say that again?"

"Nino, I'm locked inside Abbracci."

"What happened? How did you get locked inside Abbracci? How did you get my home number?"

With a slurred voice, he said that he had gone to the restroom and, having had a few drinks too many, he fell asleep on the toilet seat. Well, I thought, that is what I get for having nice restrooms.

When the gentleman woke up he was scared to death because he was in complete darkness and didn't know where he was and what he was doing there. He finally came to his senses and realized that he was still in Caffè Abbracci, in the restroom, and that everybody was gone except him. "Thank God your name was listed so I got your number. Would you please come here now and let me out?" he asked.

FERDIE: It was 1990 and Spanish director Pedro Almodóvar was in mid-controversy over the movie *Tie Me Up! Tie Me Down!* The Miami Film Festival sponsored a special showing of the movie and brought Almodóvar and other cast members to South Florida for the opening. They dined at Caffè Abbracci.

NINO: Yes, there is a very special photo which shows what happened when I presented the tab to Antonio Banderas and Victoria Abril. They "tied me up and tied me down" and stuffed the check into my pocket. The group departed with "Ciao, e tante grazie, Nino." This explains why on that July evening people who called for reservations were told, "Sorry. Nino is tied up right now!"

Nino tied up by Antonio Banderas and Victoria Abril, Caffè Abbracci, Miami, 1990. Nino Pernetti collection.

Nino and Mario Andretti, Caffè Abbracci, Miami, 2002. Nino Pernetti collection.

FERDIE: On a quiet Tuesday morning six months after Caffè Abbracci opened, you received a phone call from Oprah Winfrey's personal secretary asking if you would cater a cocktail and dinner party on the terrace of Ms. Winfrey's Fisher Island mansion for approximately thirty of her friends from Chicago.

NINO: It was two weeks before Memorial Day weekend. I was floored! Oprah Winfrey! My initial reaction was that someone was pulling my leg. But life at the restaurant had taught me to be flexible. It wasn't a joke. Oprah, the most powerful, influential TV personality in America, was asking me to take charge of her important night. My heart was beating fast and I resolved to do my super best.

In one conversation with her she said, "Nino, everything has to be elegant and first class." To which I quickly replied, "That's why you chose me." She laughed graciously.

Her personal assistant and I discussed the many details; the menu, the decor, the tablecloths, the flowers, glasses, and silverware—everything had to be white. In fact, the guests were to wear only white. The theme was "The Great Gatsby."

Oprah's assistant flew into Miami ahead of time to coordinate everything and to finalize the arrangements. The day of the event, Mauro, the chef, and I pulled up to the ferry dock. Behind us with the rented U-Haul were two cooks, four waiters, and two dishwashers.

I arrived at the mansion full of anticipation, but Oprah was not there yet. I introduced her assistant to Chef Mauro and his team and left them busily at work; I made preparations to be back at 6:30 p.m. The party was to start at 7:30. As I was going out the door, the flowers were arriving, perfuming the air with the heavenly scent of lilies and white anthuriums. When I returned the house was ready.

Finally it was time to meet Oprah Winfrey. She was beautiful, slim, and very elegant, yet she retained an informal personal style.

Dark, ominous clouds gloomily presaged rain showers that threatened to delay the dinner. Just then Oprah received a frantic phone call that her guests were stuck on the boat at the Port of Fort Lauderdale and would have to wait until the storm subsided in order to sail to Fisher Island. They were going to be late.

From apparently bad news, good things sometimes flow. We were stuck alone in the sitting room with nothing to do but talk. Imagine. Almost two hours with someone like Oprah.

The first question I asked her was, "What does Harpo

mean?" She smiled then grabbed a pen and wrote her name on a piece of paper. "Nino, read it from right to left."

She talked lovingly about the most important person in her life, the person who taught her how to read at the age of three, who gave her love and advice and told her to listen to other people and to empathize with them: her dearly loved grandmother.

I could relate because in my heart the most important person in my life was my stepmother. We swapped stories of our youth and life. I told her that although we grew up miles and years apart we shared a debt of love and gratitude to the people important in our lives. When I left that night, I felt that I had made a friend of a great lady. Sharing two special hours with this wonderful woman was a privilege.

FERDIE: Sylvester Stallone, after having eaten at Caffè Abbracci, asked you if you would send a cook to his home daily to prepare lunch and dinner for him and his family, and you provided that service while he lived in Miami.

But one of the most remarkable moments in Caffè Abbracci's history occurred on a Sunday afternoon in 2001. The lead singer of *The Phantom of the Opera*, Keith Buterbaugh, called for reservations. At that time he was performing at the Theater of Performing Arts in Fort Lauderdale. You put your marketing skills to work and called a good friend, Stan Beran, at home. He was the owner of Sound Performance, a music shop.

NINO: I asked Stan where on a Sunday could I find an electric keyboard and microphone. I explained to him who was coming to dinner and that I would eventually ask him to sing a song but needed the piano just in case he requested one and a microphone. Stan said he knew someone who could lend me the equipment for the night.

Keith Buterbaugh walked in at 7:30 with three other gentlemen. After pampering him throughout dinner and dessert, I told him that everyone in the packed dining room recognized him and that was why everyone was staring at him. Before talking to him, I had gone to each table and told everyone who he was and that I was going to ask him to sing one song. Keith, feeling all eyes on him, said, "But, Nino, I need an instrument to accompany me."

"But of course. We just happen to have an electric keyboard right here for you." Once the piano and microphone were set up, I made an announcement and Keith sang "The Music of the Night." His beautiful singing silenced the crowd; people cried, some held their loved ones and closed their eyes and listened carefully so as not to miss a note. At the end, everyone rose to their feet in a thunderous ovation for a good five minutes.

FERDIE: Caffè Abbracci was making news nationally. *Esquire* was giving it accolades; *Condé Nast Traveler* named it one of America's top 150 restaurants. *Food and Wine* and *Gourmet* featured it.

NINO: As nice as it was, I did not want to rest on my laurels. I knew I had to be there at the door greeting people every day. I wanted everyone to feel at home at Caffè Abbracci.

When Robert De Niro walked in, there was no mistaking him. Many people tell me that I look like him. But I told De Niro as I was shaking his hand and welcoming him, "So finally, you're the guy who looks like me." De Niro had a good laugh. He had his favorite dish, mozzarella caprese, and a nice plate of linguine alle vongole. I told him, "That's what Robert Redford eats, too. And De Niro replied, "Yes, but I'm better looking. I'm Italian."

And unbelievably for me, one day at Caffè Abbracci I had another amazing guest: my number-two sports idol after Pelé: Ayrton Senna, from Brazil. Each time he was in Miami on his way to Europe to race in a Formula One Grand Prix he would come and eat at Caffè Abbracci. I would pick him up from the Grand Bay Hotel, have dinner with him, and then drive him back. He was a four-time Formula One world champion, the fastest and most daring driver in the world. Tragically, Ayrton died in 1994 while racing in San Marino, Italy.

Another racing driver and famous actor who frequented Caffè Abbracci was Paul Newman. He owned a couple of race cars, and each time there was an Indy car race in Miami I knew he would come for dinner that day. On one occasion, I went to the nearest grocery store and purchased a few bottles of Newman's Own salad

Nino with Keith Buterbaugh, Caffè Abbracci, Miami, 2001. Nino Pernetti collection.

Nino with Ayrton Senna, Caffè Abbracci, 2000. Nino Pernetti collection. 1992. Photo by Luisita Sevilla Pacheco.

dressings. We served him a salad, and the waiter held up his salad dressing bottles on a tray and asked him which he would like. There was an explosion of laughter from the table. I watched that whole scenario from a few feet away then approached the table. Paul Newman shook my hand and said, "This was the best joke played on me since I've been in Miami.

But I replied very seriously, "This is not a joke. I do use these salad dressings. Why do you think I am so successful?"

Paul Newman, with another laugh, said, "That is a great line, Nino."

Don King is a regular at Caffè Abbracci; his charisma is felt the moment he steps inside the restaurant. He starts to shout in a loud voice, "Ninooooooooo,

Don King with Ferdie Pacheco in the ring.

Mike Tyson, 1998. Photo by Luisita Sevilla Pacheco.

Ninooooooo, Ninooooooo," and every patron lays down knives and forks to watch in amazement. He is a consummate showman. He goes around the restaurant and in his high-pitched voice says hello to everyone. Each waiter and busboy who crossed his path got a hundred-dollar bill along with a handshake. The atmosphere was like a circus. One day he came in with Mike Tyson. Mike wanted spaghetti with meatballs, and I said, with regret, "We don't have this."

Then Tyson said, "Bring me anything on the menu." That's when Don King smacked him on the head and told him, "What do you think this is, a zoo?"

Robin Williams must be the only non-Italian who speaks "Italian" so well. No Italian could understand him, yet his impersonation is perfect. Even I was impressed when he came in for dinner and started to gesticulate and speak in this strange Italian-sounding language. It took me a few moments to realize that the very talented Robin Williams, with his remarkable sense of humor, was ordering with such an Italian accent that it was hard not to laugh. The man is an authentic comic genius.

FERDIE: And then came Nino Benvenuti, the most popular Italian boxer of his era and welterweight/middleweight champion of Italy, 1968–69.

NINO: When this tall, handsome man who looked like a movie star walked into Caffè Abbracci I could not believe my eyes. He was a huge hero to everyone of Italian heritage. Nino Benvenuti. I seated him at the best table, served a nice Barolo, and made his entourage happy. He had with him the daughter of another Italian hero, Primo Carnera, Giovanna. They called Primo the boxer with a warm heart, and for my money that was correct.

I attended a function for the National Italian American Foundation and Tommy Lasorda (a regular at Caffè Abbracci) introduced me to Frank Sinatra in 1992. Ol' Blue Eyes Sinatra, with his boyish smile, impressed me with his many questions about Italy. He even attempted to talk to me in Italian but spoke a kind of southern dialect that I could not fully understand.

I invited Lasorda and Sinatra and a few others to come to Caffè Abbracci for a nightcap. Sinatra ended up having a couple of grappas and exchanging jokes and pleasantries with Lasorda. I could see that the two were like brothers, with Lasorda always taking the lead, which was tough to do with the likes of Frank Sinatra.

What are the chances that three of the biggest TV stars, David Letterman, Geraldo Rivera, and Peter Jennings, would be present at Caffè Abbracci at separate tables at the same time for lunch? This was a tiny lesson in how the pecking order of major TV works. I went to each table and informed each of the presence of the other two in the room.

Here is a lesson in being a gentleman. Geraldo Rivera got up and went to each table and personally greeted the others and shook hands and chatted for five minutes. The other two waved across the crowded room but nothing else. In one moment, I knew who was in control. Later, on the way out, they spoke to each other.

The great mayor, the hero of the New York. What an honor for me to receive Rudy Giuliani at Caffè Abbracci. I was mesmerized by his personality—so firm, so commanding, yet very friendly and warm. True to his Italian heritage he wanted to eat a nice plate of pasta with seafood. I told him that this was my favorite dish and added, "Mr. Giuliani, if you don't like it you have a 30-day money-back guarantee." He laughed and said the service was great, this was America.

One evening I walked in and was surprised to see Petula Clark sitting at my front table with Ferdie and Luisita. I shook her hand and said, "It's so nice to see you again, Miss Clark." She looked at me, searching my face to try to remember where we had met.

It was forty-two years ago, while she was staying in Venice's Bauer Grünwald Hotel. She was in Venice to give a concert. The concert was held in San Marco Square and was a rousing success. I brought room service to her suite afterward. I complimented her on her tour de force, and she graciously gave me front-row seats to her next performance.

Nino with Nino Benvenuti, Caffè Abbracci, Miami, 2005. Nino Pernetti collection.

Nino with Frank Sinatra at a charity function, Miami, 1992. Nino Pernetti collection.

Geraldo Rivera filming at Los Violines Supper Club with Cuban dancers Lourdes Albarellos and Cristina Suárez, Miami, 1991. Ferdie and Luisita Seville Pacheco collection.

Rudy Giuliani with Nino, Caffè Abbracci, Miami, 2006. Nino Pernetti collection.

Nino, Petula Clark, and Ferdie Pacheco, Caffè Abbracci, Miami, 2006. Photo by Luisita Sevilla Pacheco.

Tatiana and Katerina Pernetti, 2006. Photo by Nick Guillermo Pérez.

FERDIE: Nino, you have two lovely daughters, Tatiana and Katerina. Both are very healthy and lively children, and you wanted to give back to the community by joining the Jackson Memorial Foundation, specifically to help those unfortunate children born with birth defects or other incurable diseases.

NINO: My children are a gift from God; now my life is complete. After many years in Miami, my attachment to this country grew stronger and stronger and I realized that it had brought me many good things. My destiny guided me here to Miami, Florida, U.S.A. Like an old boat, I had reached my final destination. It gave me financial security and a beautiful life that I would never have achieved anywhere else. I decided to become an American citizen in the early '90s. I feel like an adopted son. It's funny. When I visit Salò, all my friends call me the American, "É arrivato l' Americano!" I am proud of my new nationality and I'm grateful for how I have been embraced.

Caffè Abbracci is always filled with satisfied customers being tended to by enthusiastic and capable staff under the direct supervision of the general manager, Loris Curzio, and his assistant, Eduardo Gutiérrez. The kitchen staff prepares the best food day after day under the leadership of executive Chef Mauro Bazzanini.

At Caffè Abbracci everybody is somebody because we truly believe that "abbiamo bisogno di mangiare, come il fiore ha bisogno dell'acqua per poter fiorire e l'aquilone del vento per poter volare!" Yes, indeed, we need food like the flower needs water to bloom and the kite, wind to fly. Could this dream happen anywhere? No, only in America!

Grazie, America!

Caffè Abbracci's staff, 2006. Photo by Derek Cole.

DESSERTS

Pears with Chocolate Sauce

Pere al Cioccolato

2½ cups granulated sugar

4 cups of water, enough to cover pears

Juice of 2 lemons

4 strips lemon rind

Pinch of cinnamon

4 medium-large Bartlett or Comice pears, underripe, peeled

5 tablespoons heavy cream

½ cup strong espresso

½ cup coarsely chopped bittersweet chocolate

1 tablespoon unsalted butter

2 tablespoons Grand Marnier

8 amarettini, coarsely chopped

4 sprigs fresh mint

15 raspberries

Combine the water and sugar in a pot just large enough to hold the 4 pears. Bring to a boil and add the lemon juice, lemon rind, and cinnamon. Boil for 5 minutes. Carefully lower the pears into the sugar syrup and cook over moderate heat for 15–20 minutes. Remove the pears from the syrup and cool.

Combine the cream and espresso in a small pan and cook over moderate heat for 4 minutes, or until mixture thickens. Add the chocolate. Stir until the chocolate melts and blends with the cream and espresso. Stir in the butter and the Grand Marnier. Cook for another 4–6 minutes, stirring constantly with a wooden spoon.

Divide the chocolate sauce evenly among 4 plates. Slice each pear into 6–8 slices and place them on the sauce. Sprinkle the amarettini on the pears. Garnish with mint and raspberries. Serves 4.

Wine pairings: Malvasia delle Lipari Passito; Bonny Doon Muscat Vin de Glaciere.

see color plate 36

Rice Pudding with Mascarpone and Pine Nuts

Budino di Riso con Mascarpone e Pignoli

½ cup pine nuts

4 ounces long-grain white rice

2 cups whole milk

1 vanilla bean

2 cinnamon sticks

2 cups cream, plus 1 tablespoon

1 cup sugar, plus 1 tablespoon

1 cup mascarpone

¼ cup candied fruit

Place the pine nuts in a small, heavy skillet over medium heat. Toast, shaking the pan or stirring frequently, until the nuts are lightly golden and fragrant, about 5 minutes. Pour on a plate to cool.

Place the rice in a heavy saucepan, stir in the milk, vanilla bean, and cinnamon sticks and bring to a simmer; cook, stirring occasionally with a wooden spoon, 25–30 minutes. Stir in the 2 cups cream and continue for another 30–35 minutes. Remove the pan from the heat, stir in 1 cup sugar, cover, and cool, about 40 minutes. Remove the cinnamon sticks and vanilla bean and add the mascarpone and candied fruit.

Preheat the oven to 350°F.

Mix the pine nuts with 1 tablespoon cream and 1 tablespoon sugar. Place them on a foil-lined baking tray and bake until lightly browned, about 3 minutes. Serve the rice pudding with a sprinkling of pine nuts. Serves 4.

Wine pairings: Malvasia delle Lipari Passito; Bonny Doon Muscat Vin de Glaciere.

Ricotta Cheesecake

Torta di Ricotta

Crust:

2 cups whole wheat flour, plus 2 tablespoons, for dusting the pan

¼ pound salted butter, plus 1 tablespoon, for greasing the pan, softened

1 cup granulated sugar

2 eggs

1¼ teaspoons orange zest

1¼ teaspoons lemon zest

Strawberry Sauce:

½ pound strawberries, hulled

3 tablespoons granulated sugar

1 whole star anise

3 teaspoons orange zest

1 tablespoon butter

¼ cup strained fresh orange juice

¼ cup dry Marsala

1½ tablespoons fresh lemon juice

Filling:

6 large eggs, separated

2 cups granulated sugar

3 teaspoons vanilla extract

2 pounds Italian ricotta, room temperature

1 pound cream cheese, room temperature

1 cup candied fruit

Crust: Combine 2 cups flour, the butter, sugar, eggs, orange and lemon zest in the bowl of an electric mixer. Mix at medium speed until the dough is nice and firm. Remove the dough from the bowl, cover with plastic wrap, and refrigerate for about 2 hours. Grease a 10-inch spring form pan with 1 tablespoon softened butter and dust it with flour. Shake off the excess flour.

While the dough is chilling, make the strawberry sauce.

Strawberry Sauce: Combine all of the sauce ingredients in a medium saucepan, bring to a boil over medium-high heat, and cook for 5 minutes. Remove the mixture from the heat, pour it into a bowl, and cover with foil. Allow the flavors to infuse for 15 minutes. Transfer the mixture to the jar of a blender and purée. Strain the sauce through a fine-mesh strainer into a bowl and refrigerate.

Remove the dough from the refrigerator and place it on a cutting board or marble countertop and flatten with a long rolling pin. Gently place the flattened dough into the greased springform pan and pat the dough onto the bottom and sides. Trim the edges.

Preheat the oven to 375°F.

Filling: Beat the egg yolks, sugar, and vanilla with a whisk in a large bowl until the yolks are a pale yellow. Add the ricotta and cream cheese and beat well. Add the candied fruit and, with a rubber spatula, fold until the fruit is completely combined. Beat the egg whites in a separate bowl until they form stiff peaks when the beaters are lifted from the bowl.

Fold half of the egg whites into the ricotta mixture. Fold in the other half in the same manner. Pour the ricotta mixture into the dough-lined pan and bake until the cake is golden brown on top and set in the center, about 2 hours.

Serve each slice with 2 tablespoons of strawberry sauce. Serves 8.

Wine pairings: Malvasia delle Lipari Passito; Bonny Doon Muscat Vin de Glaciere.

Tiramisù

⅔ cup heavy cream

3 large eggs, separated

⅓ cup granulated sugar, plus 1 tablespoon

2 cups mascarpone

½ cup coffee-flavored liqueur

1 cup strong espresso, room temperature

1 7-ounce package soft ladyfingers (such as Italian Savoiardi)

3 ounces bittersweet chocolate, grated

In a medium bowl, whip the cream until firm, then refrigerate. In a large bowl, beat the egg yolks with ⅓ cup sugar until light in color. In another bowl, with a whisk or a hand-held electric mixer, beat the egg whites to stiff peaks. Add the 1 tablespoon sugar to the whites and beat until firm. Using a rubber spatula, fold the whipped cream into the beaten yolks, then fold in the mascarpone and ⅓ of the beaten egg whites. Gently fold in the remaining egg whites.

In a small bowl, combine the espresso and coffee-flavored liqueur; set aside. Dip both sides of half of the ladyfingers in the espresso mixture and use them to line the bottom of an approximately 8x10-inch glass or ceramic baking dish. Spoon half of the cheese mixture over the ladyfingers and spread in a smooth, even layer.

Dip both sides of the remaining ladyfingers in the espresso mixture and arrange over the cheese layer. Spread the remaining cheese mixture evenly over the ladyfingers. Cover with foil and refrigerate for one day. Just before serving top with grated chocolate. Serves 6–8.

Wine pairings: Malvasia delle Lipari Passito; Bonny Doon Muscat Vin de Glaciere.

Zabaglione with Wild Berries

Zabaglione ai Frutti di Bosco

1 cup each raspberries, blackberries, mulberries, strawberries, quartered

8 large egg yolks

½ cup granulated sugar

1 cup sweet Marsala

1 cup heavy cream

4 sprigs mint, for garnish

Wash the berries under cold running water. Pat them dry with paper towels.

In a copper saucepan or bowl, combine the egg yolks and sugar and whisk until foamy, then set the saucepan or bowl over a pot of gently simmering water (or use a double boiler). Continue whisking until the yolks start to thicken. Add the Marsala and whisk constantly until the mixture doubles in volume, 4–5 minutes. Do not let the mixture boil or the eggs will curdle. Transfer the mixture to a bowl and refrigerate about 2 hours. Before serving, whip the cream and fold it into the egg yolk mixture thoroughly. Divide the zabaglione evenly among 4 plates and top with berries. Garnish with a mint sprig. Serves 4.

Wine pairings: Malvasia delle Lipari Passito; Bonny Doon Muscat Vin de Glaciere.

see color plate 37

INDEX

Gaiga, Raoul, 212, *212*
Garlic: in Korean food, 124–25; mashed potatoes, 223; roasted, 53
Gautier, Claude, 141
Germany: Frankfurt, 47, 65–66; Hanover, 63–64
Giuliani, Rudy, 249, *250*
Goat cheese: cured beef with, 26; and pear salad, 58; shrimp with tomatoes and, 153; with pine nuts and sun-dried tomatoes, 28
Gorgonzola: oysters with, 31; polenta with shiitake mushrooms and, 32
Grand Hotel Bristol, 45
Grapes: risotto with, 114
Grouper: with black olives and tomatoes, 150
Il Guelfo Bianco, 65

Hanover, Germany, 63–64
Hari Raya Puasa, 166
Honey, 70
Hospitality, 1
Hotel Wilder Mann, 64–65, *65*
Humidity, 163
Hunting, 105–6

Iglesias, Julio, 137–40, *138*
InterContinental Hotels, 63, 103. *See also* InterContinental Mosi-Oa-Tunya Hotel; Lusaka InterContinental Hotel
InterContinental Mosi-Oa-Tunya Hotel, 107
Island of Penang, 167–68
Istanbul: cuisine of, 176–77; Grand Bazaar of, 175
Istanbul Sheraton Hotel, 174–77, *177*; patrons of, 176; staff of, 175
Italian sausage. *See* Sausage
Italy: Campione, 10–15; Peschiera, 14–16; postwar, 5–20; Salò, 41–48

Jackson Memorial Foundation, 251
Jackson, Michael, 204
Jennings, Peter, 249
Jones, Tom, 137–38

Kabul, Afghanistan, 78, 81, *100*, 101–4, *103–4*
Kimchee, 124–25

King, Don, 247–48
Kissinger, Henry, 172
Korean food, 124–25
Kota Beldames Baser, 166
Kuala Lumpur, Malaysia, 143, 163–71, *164–65, 169–71*

Lamb: chops with dried cherries and berries, 186; tenderloin with Marsala, 185
Lentil and tomato soup, 55
Letterman, David, 249
Linguine: with clams, 90; with shrimp, 91
Livers. *See* Chicken livers
Locanda Gemma, 18–19, 44, *48*
Lokanta, 176
Los Roques, 203
Lusaka InterContinental Hotel, 105

Machorro, Manuel, 141–42
Mahi mahi with lemon and capers, 151
Malaysia: culinary customs in, 166–67; ethnic groups in, 163–64; festivals in, 166; humidity in, 163; Kuala Lumpur, 143, 163–71, *164–65, 169–71*; religious mix in, 163
Manor House Hotel, *66*, 67
Manzanero, Armando, *142*
Marinade: anchovy-balsamic, 154
Marinara sauce, 59
Marsala: lamb tenderloin with, 185; veal chops with grapes and, 190
Martinet, Pierre, 102
Mascarpone: rice pudding with pine nuts and, 256
Mason, Gary, 203–4
Mastroianni, Marcello, 216
Meat: beef tenderloin with aromatic herbs, 182; beef tenderloin with black pepper sauce, 183; lamb chops with dried cherries and berries, 186; lamb tenderloin with Marsala, 185; pork tenderloins with applesauce, 187; pork tenderloins with balsamic-plum sauce, 188; pork tenderloins with wild mushrooms, 189; salt-baked beef tenderloin, 184; sirloin steak with gorgonzola sauce, 181; sweet-and-sour veal scaloppine, 196; veal chops with grapes and Marsala, 190; veal scaloppine

coffee in, 201–2; Los Roques, 203; nightlife in, 202

Villa Alba, 44

Villa Vera Tennis Club, 135, 137–38

Vollari, Vittorio, 141

Whiskey, 199–200

White truffle, 119; oil, 152

Wiesel, Elie, *233*

Williams, Robin, 248

Wine: from Chianti, 15; chicken with balsamic vinegar and red wine, 131; snails with anchovies and red wine, 39; tasting, 215; tilapia with truffle oil and white wine, 156

Winfrey, Oprah, 244–45

Yellowtail: grilled with sun-dried tomatoes, 161; with artichokes, 159; with fennel and tomatoes, 160

Yogurt, penne with pumpkin and, 96

Zabaglione with wild berries, 259

Zambia, 105, *107*, 107–9; crafts market in, 109

Zucchini: soup, 56; stuffed, 229

NINO PERNETTI

Every evening at 6:00 p.m. the doors open to the lobby of Caffè Abbracci in Coral Gables, where numerous awards and restaurant reviews recognizing it as one of the finest Italian restaurants in South Florida are displayed. Owner Nino Pernetti is there to greet every customer with a warm handshake. On any given evening, inside you will find a potpourri of locals and international diners indulging in Caffè Abbracci's Venetian specialties. Nino has a way of making them all feel like family.

How did Nino Pernetti create such a standout in the flock of fine Italian restaurants that South Florida offers? The magic he weaves is not an overnight sensation. Nino has honed his considerable skills in the restaurant and hospitality business all of his life.

He was born in Campione, Lago di Garda, Italy. There, at age thirteen, Nino got his first job in a restaurant, Locanda Gemma making espressos and cappuccinos. He was hooked, as he loved seeing the smiles on his customers' faces. When Nino finished high school, he burned with ambition to become a restauranteur. He enrolled in hotel school at Gardone Riviera on the spectacular Garda Lake in northern Italy and graduated with honors. While in school, during summer holidays he worked at the elegant Bauer-Grünwald Hotel and the fashionable Grand Hotel Bristol in Merano. The rest is history.

Nino's hospitality career has included executive positions in some of the finest hotels and resorts in the world. He worked for InterContinental Hotels, Americana Hotels, and Sheraton International, in Germany, England, Eleuthera, Kabul, Lusaka, Livingstone, Seoul, Acapulco, Singapore, Kuala Lumpur, Brussels, Istanbul, Caracas, and Paris. It doesn't hurt that Nino speaks fluent French, German, Spanish, Portuguese, and English, in addition to his native Italian. He is a man of style and taste, which is reflected in everything he does: "If you want to run a fine restaurant, you must first learn every phase of the business, and when you feel like you know it well, you must sacrifice yourself to being there personally seven days a week. Then and only then can you hope to be a success."

He picked out the best design from a designer who understood what he wanted. The firm, Deco-Tech Architectural Design, belongs to Giorgio Bibolini, Nino's former partner. Nino gave instructions; Giorgio drew up plans. Nino made notes about napkins, designer dinnerware, unusual silverware, and wineglasses on scraps of paper. He wanted the restaurant to feel like a theater, like an elegant yet unpretentious apartment. With Caffè Abbracci he could add a real bar, a separate space but part of the other room, with a shared design integrated by color. Nino said his restrooms would be the best in town; he fretted over the uniforms of the parking attendants. He supervised every detail. He meant to have an ideal restaurant, and in time he had just that.

The food, the menu, the wine—here was Nino's chief area of expertise. A well-deserved reputation gained from worldwide travels was based on his encyclopedic knowledge of food.

Nino's philosophy is simple: "I do not want to serve huge quantities of food so that the customer feels stuffed when he leaves. Our food is light, and the main thing is the flavor. We want our customers to leave satisfied but not stuffed. Around my town in Italy this is the way we eat. You do not see fat Italians there. It is what we want for our customers here: light but good tasting. Taste everything, even the cooking wines. What we use here is the wine I drink myself. Also surround yourself with the best—the best cooks, the best waiters, and train them well. But they must eat before they work, because I know as a child who went hungry that that is very important, because they will be grumpy and not work well if they do not have a full stomach."

Nino is an avid reader, and his residence is brimming with an incredible collection of antiques, art, and Venetian glass, which he has assembled from all the wonderful places he has lived. He is an active man who loves to play tennis, water-ski, and, most recently, snow-ski. He has two daughters, Tatiana and Katerina. Regularly Nino brings Tatiana to the restaurant to familiarize her with the customers, and to start to understand and learn the restaurant business. She puts on an apron and loves it, and so do the customers.

Nino is also dedicated to his community. He serves on the boards of the Jackson Memorial Foundation, the Miami Symphony Orchestra, and the Concert Association of Florida and was chairperson of the Jackson Metropolitans support group of the Jackson Memorial Foundation.

FERDIE PACHECO

Ferdie Pacheco, M.D., has been called a Renaissance man because of his multifaceted career. He has been successful as a pharmacist, a medical doctor, and a fight doctor, including working as a corner man for twelve world champions, among them, Muhammad Ali, for seventeen years. He has also worked as a boxing commentator for NBC, Showtime, and Univisión and has won two Emmys, in a total of twenty-five years on television. He has had fourteen books published and has written articles, columns, and reviews for Florida magazines and newspapers. He is a world-recognized painter and has focused many of his works on Florida history, specializing in Ybor City, where he was born of Spanish parents. He helped finance his medical education by contributing cartoons to major national magazines.

He has been exhibiting his work in galleries since 1983. He won the gold medal and first prize in Tonneins, France, 1987, and the best colorist award at the Musée du Luxembourg in Paris, 1990. His paintings are in the collections of many famous personalities, such as Andy García, Shirley MacLaine, Budd Schulberg, Petula Clark, Ernest Borgnine, and Evander Holyfield.

He has sold six scripts to major studios, and a documentary of his life, *Ferdie Pacheco: The World of the Fight Doctor*, has been shown in film festivals.

He has written the following novels, which are yet unpublished: "The Making of a Don" (The Legend of the Black Rooster), a Mafia novel set in the South (Ybor City) in 1940; "Lucy Jay and the Medal," based on the true story of a woman doctor who wins the Congressional Medal of Honor only to have it taken back; "The Lector," a sweeping story about a cigar factory that takes place between 1910 and 1940; and "Sweet Sam," the story of a New Orleans jazz musician.

LUISITA SEVILLA PACHECO

Luisita Sevilla (Karen Louise Maestas) was born and raised in Denver, Colorado.

Luisita has been dancing her whole life. In the 1950s she danced the jitterbug, but always dreamed of being a Spanish dancer. The opportunity came in 1959 when José Greco was giving a dance performance in Denver. Although she was only fifteen, Karen auditioned for his troupe. Greco told her that she was very talented but that she needed to learn technique. The only place to do that was in Spain, in particular, the city of Sevilla.

Karen told her mother that she was going to Spain, even if she had to swim across the ocean. Her parents, Joe and Margo Maestas, believed in her so much that they sold their life insurance to finance the trip. The next month Karen was in Spain and within a year she had become a professional flamenco dancer, newly renamed Luisita Sevilla because no one in Sevilla could pronounce her real name.

For twelve years she traveled through Europe, South America, Asia, Malaysia, Australia, New Zealand, and Japan doing what she loved most.

She met Ferdie Pacheco in Miami, Florida, in 1969. They fell in love and married in 1970. She opened a dance studio and taught all forms of Spanish dance. Their daughter, Tina, is a respected movie editor.

Luisita is also a painter, a published photographer, and an author. In 1988, she wrote and published *Bobby Lorca: A Tribute to a Flamenco Dancer*. This book of stories, photographs, and poetry was dedicated to the memory of her deceased dance partner who succumbed to AIDS earlier that year. Proceeds from the book were donated to fund AIDS research.

She is now retired from dance and is proud to have shared her talent with young dancers who have become professional flamenco dancers and teachers who are keeping her legacy alive. For twenty-five years she has been an active member of Children's Resources, an organization that helps abused and mentally challenged children, as a founder and past-president. A well-known Miami hostess, she loves to cook and enjoyed working with Nino Pernetti on this book.

Other Books by Ferdie Pacheco:

Blood in My Coffee: The Life of the Fight Doctor.
Sports Publishing, L.L.C. Champaign, Ill., 2005.

*The Christmas Eve Cookbook: With Tales of Noche-
buena and Chanukah*, with Luisita Sevilla Pacheco.
Gainesville: University Press of Florida, 1998.

The Columbia Restaurant Spanish Cookbook, with Adela
Hernández Gonzmart. Gainesville: University Press of
Florida, 1995.

Fight Doctor. New York: Simon and Schuster, 1977.

Fight Doctor. London: Stanley Paul & Co. Ltd.,
Hutchinson Publishing Group, 1978.

Muhammad Ali: A View from the Corner. New York:
Carol Publishing, 1992.

Pacheco's Art of the Cubans in Exile. Miami: Avanticase-
Hoyt, 2000.

Pacheco's Art of Ybor City. Gainesville: University Press of
Florida, 1997.

Renegade Lightning, with Robert Skimin. Novato, Calif.:
Presidio Press, Lyford Books, 1992.

The Trolley-Kat Alphabet. Hillsborough, Fla.:
Hillsborough Press, 2001.

The Trolley Kat Travels. Hillsborough, Fla.: Hillsborough
Press, 2001.

The 12 Greatest Rounds of Boxing: The Untold Stories.
Kingston, N.Y.: Total/Sports Illustrated, 2000.

Whos Is Artie Shaw . . . and Why Is He Following Me?
Indianapolis: AuthorHouse, 2005.

Who Killed Patton? Indianapolis: AuthorHouse, 2004.

Ybor City Chronicles: A Memoir. Gainesville: University
Press of Florida, 1994.